TO GAIL

thank you ありがとう

和子

Japanese wife

kazuko

ISBN13:978-1468022988
ISBN139781468022988

Introduction

I came to America about 40 years ago at that time very few Japanese immigrants were here. I thought we have to keep very quiet and not make any waves. That I was told. I did not have rights in America and I am not valued by American society even though I was a green card holder.

I was not treated fairly but I kept silent. My voice was never heard because I was told I was not important here America. At that time I believed there were no helpful organizations. I did no t know where or how to get any help.

I remember, one cold winter when we (my son 11 and my daughter 1) were forced to leave our rented house. I was only one week behind in rent payment. I went to the court house. the judge told me "lady if you can't pay the rent you have to get out from you're renting right away ." I still hear his voice from time to time. that irritated voice stays in my mind.

So my children and I slept on the street cold winter for three days in the snow while the wind blew so hard. We slept on the ground without any blankets.

Then the welfare tried to take my two children away from me because I was poor and I couldn't provide them shelter. Of course I did fight. These things were happening one thing after other happened to me almost every day. Because lack of knowledge of American customs, culture, law. Prejudices, my right and lack of support.

Here in America my life was not easy. But I did my best to keep quiet to try to understand American culture, to learn to be a better immigrants and to work hard. I wanted to the American people to like me and my family.

I worked whatever available job from dishwasher to cleaner to waitress to apple picker and more. When I worked at the restaurant I remember I only received .75 cent an hour. I worked many jobs and I took the money little as they paid. It was so difficult to find any jobs. Once an employer heard my accent, they would not give me any job. That was a very common experience.

When I experienced how terrible injustice and unkind people here in America treated me I felt sad and I cried a lot. I did not realize how cruel American could be.

I realized how very different the two cultures were and how different the thinking. It was much more different here than in Japan. So, I started writing my frustrations at all that happened time after time, and I remember things. That sometime made me cry. Even now, when I think about what happened to me it makes me cry. I try to understand why I was treated so differently, life here in America was so hard and painful live, but I did live through. I had these opportunity to become the woman I am today. Writing my story in my second language –English was a very challenge.
Now I write my experiences in America how painful it was living without help without understanding English, without knowing the culture and all the different ways people in America think.
I also want to introduce how I was growing up and how I learned to treat people and to have self discipline, and why we do, the way we do and think. I want to introduce the school system in Japan.

In Japan all the children learn from parents and teachers. The Japanese mother works so hard for her children to learn. Japanese parents and the teachers communicated well. Parents strongly trust the children's teachers. Also I will point out how differently Japanese women and American women think and act. I write side by side to explain the difference between why we do things and the way we do, also about employee to employer how they treat each other, and I write about old fashioned Japanese culture. But I always in my heart I am a Japanese wife.

I write three part.
One is in Florida and second will be in Massachusetts and third will be in New Hampshire

I started working on my story almost 20 years ago. My English was very bad then. But as the years have gone by my English has improved. I did not want to lose myself by packaging my story in a neat grammatically correct package. So I decided to leave it as is, because I wanted you to join me in my journey.

This is my first story.

CONTENTS

Special thanks

Elaine Habrekamp
Kathy Drexel
Marjorie Rudolph

Thank you for all your support without you I never made this book.

I RUN AWAY

Good morning sunshine. Today is a beautiful sunny day. The sky is crystal clear; the wind blows so softly, touching the tip of the leaves dancing around the trees. It is very quiet, a very peaceful time.

I sit at the kitchen table. I put my coffee cup on the table full with coffee I have just made this morning. The smell is refreshing. Steam jumps out from my cup and makes a curl going up to the ceiling and then disappears into the air. My hands hug my coffee cup, I feel warm. Warmth goes from the tip of my fingers to my arm and warms up my day.

I look out the window, what a nice and wonderful time. What a peaceful, beautiful morning. A few kids appear here and there, walking to school.

I really love to watch the children in the trailer park happy, laughing and jumping around, they try so hard to be happy and have fun. They look so innocent. They walk to school every morning.

It's a wonderful world. Watch the children gives me a moment of peace, for a little while brings me to a safe place.

Recently, I become aware of the children in the trailer park. Some kids walk across the street from my trailer holding their lunch boxes. All of a sudden the kids become bunch groups walking, running, laughing and talking They make such a happy noise.

Some kids swing their lunch boxes around bouncing them back and forth. Some kids swing them making a small loop in the air and make sounds like remote control airplanes.

Some were laughing. Some were running. Some were walking straight, some were walking zigzags, and some were chasing each other.

Some kids were already opening their lunch boxes, and were looking inside to find out today's goodies. Some kids switched lunch boxes. Some were trying to trade their sandwiches. Some are holding hands with their friends. But one kid just looked down on the road like hiding from everybody and rushed into school.

I keep on looking at them. What a peaceful time! But I am watching them too long, I forget I had a cup of coffee and my coffee is cold.

It is a beautiful sunshine and peaceful morning.

In Japan the school system was very

different than in America's. There were 60 to 65 students in one class. School hours were nine hours a day from Monday to Friday. Saturday was a half-day.

We couldn't have breaks between classes. The teachers came to our classes instead of students moving around.

Usually the teacher was outside of the class waiting for the other teacher to leave, so we did not miss a minute of our time. When each teacher came to our class to teach, we all stood up and paid respect (bowed) and said "good morning or good afternoon teacher" to them before we started class then after class was over we stood up again and bowed, we said thank you teacher. Every class we have to do this.

We still had time to pull pranks if we wanted to, but we had too much respect for our teachers. We never thought of pulling some joke on our powerful teachers. We treated our teachers like Gods. They were of the highest level. We wouldn't dare argue back. We obeyed we honored.

In the school, we didn't have a locker to put personal stuff in. We had to carry our text books, notebooks, pencils, lunch and other things needed for school every day. They were heavy!

When we arrived at school, first thing in the morning all students changed their clothes to exercise clothes and met on the playground. No matter, if it was winter or summer we had wear exercise clothes, a *bloomer (Japanese style of short pant* end of the shorts had elastic). Top we wear short sleeve shirt.

How cold in the winter we had to wear exercise clothe and stand still to listen the principal's speech every day, and then recorded music started.

We had to do our exercises all together with music for about an hour from Monday to Saturday. Then we went back to our classrooms, and then we had to change clothes again to our uniforms.

When the class was over, we went home. We changed clothes, had dinner, then we had to go to *Juku*. This was another school to get extra education, like speaking and writing English, *Shuji* write with sumi, *Ikebana* flower arrangement. *Odori* Japanese dance, Tea ceremony, *Soroban (*abacus) Japanese calculation, *Kendo, Judo* and other various lessons. *Juku* usually 5 days a week some students go to *juku* on Saturday and Sunday too.

These classes were over around 9: 00 PM.

When we arrived at home, we had to finish our home work for tomorrow's classes. We stay up until finished our homework. No excuse not to do homework.

When I was a student in Japan, I wore a dark boring colored uniform with old fashioned, ugly, uncomfortable, polished black leather shoes.

We wore ankle high, snow white socks, never, mixed with any other colors always simple, bright white socks. Such bright snow white socks reflected the sunshine and gave a nice contrast to my black shoes.

The shoes were polished every day after school. They were polished like a mirror and you could see your face in them. And we put them neatly on the floor ready for tomorrow.

Also I carried an old fashioned rectangular, black, leather bag to school. Doctors or nerd students, used to put their papers in leather bags that were very ugly.
I hated it.

Students were prohibited from wearing their hair ornaments, like hair ribbons or hair pins with bright colors.

We were only allowed to wear black hair pins or black rubber string to hold our hair. We couldn't have our hair permed.

In Japan, students wore only boring, dark-colored uniforms from kindergarten to high school.

A girl's uniform had a pleated skirt and a blouse with a sailor styled collar and three stripes around the edge with necktie.

Boys wore trousers with a high collared neck shirt and the front had medium-sized golden color metal buttons.

I believe that even now, Japanese students wear ugly uniforms of a dark color.

But in the university they wore *Kimonos with Hakama* (Japanese style trouser for woman and man). I do not know now if they still wear those *Hakama* or not.

In Japan, each school had similar design requirements but a slightly different style.

The school's logo badge was worn on their uniform's upper left near the heart. The badges represented the different schools.

Colors of the uniforms were only shades Of dark blue, navy blue or black. We did not use red, pink, yellow or other such bright colors.

In Japan students were very proud of their own uniforms. They took good care of their uniforms. They kept the uniforms clean.

The student's skirts or pants were always pressed. The pleats were sharp as razor blades.

American students wear different kinds of clothes. Some are colorful, some are plain.

This morning, I saw one girl who was clad in pink, flower printed and light green dress. Her hair was neatly tied in a ponytail with a pink ribbon wrapped around her ponytail.

She seemed very happy and loveable. She looked like a typical child. I think she was the best dresser among all the students.

Another girl wore a white blouse with lace trim around the neck. It was so refreshing and clean looking with her pink colored pants. Some were wearing sandals, some wore sneakers.

I remember what I used to do before

I went to bed. I had to lay my pleated skirt between the *tatami*(rectangular straw mats 3"x7" and inch thick that lay on the floor) and the *futon* Then, I got into the *futon*.

A *futon* is a Japanese bed similar to an American comforter. We used 100 % cotton inside our *futons.*

The *futon* was put inside a sack and then a white cover, like a bed sheet was put over the sack. So you could wash this cover frequently to keep clean.

The top was the same 100 % cotton in the sack and have covered the sack the same as the bottom of the futon. It is like an American sleeping bag.

I slept In between these covers on the *futon* that lay on the floor. I slept all night.

When I got up the next morning, my skirt's pleats were perfectly pressed, single lines, like a razor blade.

Sometimes girls would move too much while they were sleeping had double pleats in the morning. We used to pick on them and laugh but not a mean laugh.

Not every girl was as good with her pleats as I was. If your skirt has double pleats represented to us, the bad manners and disrespect or embarrassment to your mother.

We were taught that women, who moved around too much, especially while sleeping, did not have good manners.

I heard that in old-fashioned times, some women tied their feet before they went sleep so they couldn't move while sleeping.

We Japanese women grow up to be very quiet and motionless that we believed. We always keep quiet and calm.

Women were told that a woman did not rush, did not speak too loudly and did not express strong emotions or yourself.

She always kept herself quiet. That was the way Japanese women should be.

Therefore we girls were considered little

women. We started teaching a girl early to behave like a women.

When we laughed, we had to cover our mouths with our hand. We did not show our wide open mouths in the public. If we did not cover our mouths, when we laughed or yawned that was a very bad manners and a disgrace to their family.

I remember my husband telling me, when we were in Japan. When I laughed, he saw that I always covered my mouth out of habit.

"You have such a beautiful smile why do you cover your mouth when you laugh? You should not cover your mouth." he said with his warm smiling face.

When I watched the school kids from my window that morning, my memories of Japan rush out just like it had happened yesterday. As I looked at them, they made me feel at peace, making me forget time, bringing me to a safe place.

I loved watching them. I was watching the

kids for so long I forgot the time, and I forgot I had coffee in my hand.

As I mention before, we (Japanese) believed in "silence of beauty." Japanese women were expected to grow up to be very quiet and motionless.

We were supposed to not hear, not see and not speak. We call this *sambiki no salu* (Three monkeys). We always keep quiet and calm. That's the way we believe.

I used to believe that women should be well-proportioned, graceful and dainty educated and have patience, kindness and humility.

Women should always be exquisite, act calmly, and be dexterous and moderate in their action. Women should not jump around, should not be dynamic and should not be elite.

A woman should always keep herself graceful, elegant and beautiful. When she is around you, you should hardly notice she is there. When she moves, like air, you did not notice her motion and should be always beautiful. That is good manners and attractive to Japanese people.

Every morning I made lunch boxes for his children, Nancy, Tom and Jack. I also gave them each a few dollars to spend.

I made special treats for them every morning for their breakfast.

I always believed a good breakfast was a very important way to start the day.

I tried to pay a lot of attention and make sure the children had a good breakfast. I always gave them those fresh fruit to start, then few slice of bacon or sausages and eggs or French toast.

Other days I made a breakfast of fresh strawberry pancakes. I picked the strawberries. But they hated my cooking.

They told me (especially Nancy)"Kazuko what is this? You call these pancakes? These pancakes have too much red color in them.

You should not put in so many strawberries!" Or, she said, "I do not like your cooking, it's weird."

Nancy thought I would poison them.

Nancy told her grandmother, that I was poisoning them and trying to kill them, because I created ways to use vegetables in cooking. She thought the vegetables I used were some kind of weeds. That would cause them to die.

I noticed Bob's children did not like any fresh fruits or vegetables.

When I used to squeeze fresh orange Juice for them to drink, Nancy said,

"Does this juice have some poison in it? It tastes funny."

I was shocked! I told them, "Nothing is in it. Only fresh-squeezed orange juice and it is good for you. Fruit would make your skin smooth and make you pretty." I tried to be humor.

I tried to think of ways to put in fresh

fruits or chop up vegetables to mix with sauce or other foods when cooking supper for them. That way the children would not know what kind of vegetables they were eating. Sometimes I surprised myself with my creations.

What a good job I did to put vegetables in their food! I was never appreciated, of course, I realized.

When I cooked food for Bob's children, and created ways for the children to have vegetables, it was not all right with Linda (my husband's mother). She used to tell me, "My grandchildren should eat meat and potatoes. Do not trick them.

They're not rabbits or any other animal. Do not feed them any other food. You do not know anything. You are so dumb and stupid.

Well, I thought I was doing them a favor. I had made them to eat vegetables, and I had tried so hard, but I failed again. I did not know what to do. Didn't I know the American way? I hoped so. I wanted to learn quickly "so-called" American ways, so they would not call me stupid.

I tried very hard to please them from morning to night. Even when I was sleeping, I saw myself trying to please them, especially his mother.

I tried to make sure Bob's children always wore clean, starched clothes that looked like they just came from the dry cleaners.

They looked very sharp and very clean. They looked so intelligent. Bob's kids always looked very neat and very nice. Many my neighbors told me so.

The children's hair was combed every day, especially Nancy's hair.

Nancy had thick, long hair and a freckle face with a big nose. Her hair was thick.
It was very difficult to comb and always tangled. It took me a long, long time to make her hairdo.

I tied her hair into a pony tail and always

had a nice cute ribbon around her pony tail. While I was combing her hair she told me,

"you try to hurt me on purpose. You enjoy giving me pain don't you? I will tell my grandmother you hurt me." She loved to make up many stories. She liked to make trouble for me all the time. She was an evil little child, telling her grandmother and the neighbors how evil I was.

When she spoke to me she pointed at me with her finger and yelled. She never spoke To me softly.

But Bob's children looked like typical kids. One morning they were sitting on the couch watching television, waiting for the time to go to school. I was waiting too.

They looked very innocent. They looked very good, and then I would happen to see something evil in Nancy's eyes that made the ice water run though in my body.

I got up early every morning. As a matter of fact I couldn't sleep any more.

Every night I lay on the bed and closed my eyes and tried to sleep but I couldn't. My eyes stayed wide open. My ears were like those of a small animal in the woods.

I was afraid my husband's family would come after me to hurt me, like some hunter comes into the woods to go after small animals and hurt them.

I felt I was a small animal in a cage, and I tried to catch every small sound; I did not want to miss any noise.

I was like a little animal in the woods watching the hunter walk into the woods to hurt me. Like some hunter entering the wood to hurt the animals.

I was afraid Bob's sister came to my place any time she wanted. She would help herself to my special things.

I had brought many packages of clothes, jewelries and some ornaments from Japan.

She always took my things, especially jewelry and money without asking me and never returned the jewelry or money to me.

I used to leave money and jewelry in my bedroom. I never had the experience of mistrusting somebody in my country Japan.

I thought nobody would walk into my bedroom without my permission and steal my personal things? I found out this rule was not for them.

Bob's sister would bring her two babies and drop them off without asking me.

I did not mind taking care of her babies, but she complained and criticized me when I took care of her babies."You don't know how to take care of my babies. You don't do it right." That she would say.

When she came to my house, she brought a 6-pack of beer. She sat down in my kitchen chair or on the couch and started drinking her beer. When she finished, she opened my refrigerator and without asking me started drinking the beer I had bought for my husband. She would not stop drinking beer until all the beer was gone.

When it came to drinking beer, it didn't matter to her what time of the day it was, morning or night.

When she drank she spilled it all over the couch and floor, and she never tried to clean up her mess.

She left her empty bottles and cans here and there. She never tried to throw empty bottles in the trash can.

Then when she smoked cigarettes, her cigarette butts and ashes were dropped on the floor.

Even if I had just washed my floor on my hands and knees, (I did not own a mop) she never tried to pick them up or tried to help me clean.

I did not want to leave any mess because Linda would have an excuse to scold me. Also, I did not like a messy house. We Japanese never leave any messes anywhere. We are super clean people.

When she got hungry she would say to me, “Do you have any good food to eat.”

She would go to the kitchen, open my refrigerator and start to help herself without asking me. She tried to eat my food from the stove without putting the food into a dish, I started cooking from the morning. When she ate my food with a spoon from the pot and she put the same spoon back into the same pot. Oh my! That was dirty! It was disgusting.

We never, never, put back same spoon once someone had it is his mouth.

In Japan whoever ate from a spoon and put the same spoon back into the pot was prohibited and many people were throw a way that food. We were very strict about cleanliness. We did not use the cooking spoon for a taste.

We took some food, put it in a dish and then we tasted it.

When my husband’s sister ate, she would leave dirty dishes on my kitchen table, and then she took the rest of my food home without asking me. It didn't matter if we had enough food or not.

I was afraid that maybe someday a lady would come to my house to tell me my husband was in jail again. My husband often seemed to get in jail and he would need money to bail him out.

I did ask this lady, "How much do you need to bail him out."She said "three hundred dollars will do."I always gave a woman the money she asked for.

I found out later she was my husband's girl friend too. I knew then maybe I wouldn't see him for a few days. My husband and his girl friend often took a few days off. They would take a short trip somewhere, until their money was gone, as usual.

I could manage if he didn't come home for a few days or few months, but I did not like him to leave me alone with his mother and his children.

Should I have to face his mother and his children alone? I did not like to deal with his family alone. He brought me here from a safe, warm, happy and peaceful place, and he tried to drop me off in the middle of the Hell. Why didn't he kill me first? I would rather die.

I was afraid to doze anytime during the day. Bob's mother would come to my house without calling me at any time from early morning until late at night.

She would scold me, "How come you are such a lazy and miserable woman? You sleep all the time. Don't you have anything to do? You do not know how to take care of his children. You do not know how to take care of your husband. You make him drink, but you don't know how to make him stop. You are such useless! Why don't you make him stop drinking?"

I could see her hateful furious face very clearly, even while I was sleeping.

I always felt her hate made me choke.

Why was she so unhappy and full of grief? Why did she make people miserable? Didn't she know how to smile?

She was a very domineering woman. She always told people what to do, especially me. She made sure she let me know what I did wrong, how stupid I was and how useless I was. She thought she was always right.

I think she was miserable herself. She was a very unhappy and nosey person. She could not stand to see other people's happiness.

She was very successful at making other people miserable. She was a wicked witch. Maybe Hell sent her back to this world.

She tried very hard to find some excuse to scold me. She loved to make me cry. She enjoyed seeing me miserable.

It seemed like she did not have any other thing to do. Was her only entertainment making me cry? Making me sad? I believed. She really enjoyed my misery. The more miserable I got the better mood she was in. It is a terrible thing to live with fear every day.

I developed a sleeping disorder at during these days. I become paranoid. Any small sound, like a whisper made me jump and kept me wake.

I was not able to have peaceful, good sleep at all. My mind was shut down.

My emotions were very deep and dark, like stormy waters in an angry ocean. The waves were so high they almost reached to the sky. They came and went. When the waves were gone they left me dirty, nasty and filled with sad memorized. There was never any peace in my heart.

This disturbed me. It made me panic and scared. I did not feel pain any more. I did not have any emotions, and my tears were dried out with nothing left to cry.

I had tried so hard to please his family but nothing was ever good enough for them, I realize. It was very simple. Bob's family just hated me so much.

They would do anything to hurt me. She tried very hard, and she seemed to enjoy hurting me. I did not know what I should do to please them anymore. I felt lost.

When I first arrived in this country, I was naïve and I had a lot of trust in his family. I was ready to work hard for them even on our honeymoon, and I tried every possible way to work for them, but that energy was used up and nothing left inside me. I was lost.

My trust, respect and feelings for them were gone. Where it had gone? How it had happened? I didn't know. I wished I could know. I wished I get it back.

Being Japanese, I had to do my duty no matter what happens. Believe me I did everything you could think of.

Being Japanese we could adjusted any situation very well. I did try very hard to be a proud Japanese wife.

I thought my duty was I got up early in the morning every day. I cooked dinner for Linda and my husband and his children. I took care of his children extremely well. I cleaned his mother's double sized trailer and our single sized trailer. I babysat for his sister's babies and did her chores. I worked very hard every day, but I lost any feelings toward them.

Every day I worked for them, but I worked without emotion, like a zombie.

After I came to this country, I could not remember when I had a good sleep or a good laugh and enough food to eat even when I was pregnant.

I wished just one day I could have a good deep sleep and not have to think about Bob's family. I wanted to go into a deep sleep and never wake up. I hoped tomorrow would never come.

It would be wonderful if I never woke up.

How wonderful and peaceful for me to sleep forever!

I wanted to leave this world and be without fear, or memory, and I wanted to forget everything about this life. How wonderful it would be! I wished I could sleep now.

I thought about taking my life away many times, but deep inside some little voice told me I could not take my life away. I must keep working and be patient. A sunny day will come.

But on the other hand I had to face the evil child Nancy. When I was thinking about her it made frigid my bones and cold run though my spine.

Bob's three children were not angels at all. They were brought up with hate. They had no love, no trust. They stole. They were lazy and lied. Nancy stole money, jewelry and clothes. Whenever she touched my things, they disappeared.

Linda came to my place to tell me about kids' behavior in the trailer park.

If they caused any trouble, it was my fault, because I did not teach them better behavior. She would say that.

Bob's pay checks were sent to my mother-in-law directly.

She never explained why my husband's money was sent directly to her, and I did not ask why, because I was polite Japanese wife. We (Japanese) never asked about money.

She also said, "I did not need any personal items, because I had brought things from Japan more than enough. I stayed home and cleaned and took care of the children so I did not need any fancy things to wear."

When I was in Japan I wore very expensive, fancy clothes and shoes all my life. I never wore cheap rags. I lived in high society.

Linda got everything she wanted, but she was never happy, when I bought the children's clothes even though I shopped with money from my mother in Japan Linda complained, what I bought and how I did about children clothes.

For example, the clothes colors are too bright or too dark. It looked not comfortable. They look ugly and cheap."

She told me, "The style is too old-fashioned. The skirt's length is too short or too long." They were never right, because I had bought them clothes.

She said, "You never pay good money for his children clothe or not pay attention what they want or need and make them look cheap. Can't you pay more attention and get them better clothes? They are my grandchildren. I won't make them wear these clothes and look like clowns!"

Even if I tried to buy very expensive or very beautiful clothes, it didn't matter. It just gave her another reason to scold me. When the children came home from school, they changed to play clothes. Even in their play clothes I made sure to put starch and ironed their clothes and double checked to make sure they did not have any wrinkles or faded colors.

I tried hard to keep their clothes looked like brand new, but Linda always said,

"Why aren't their clothes pressed or look faded and so dirty? Don't you use starch?" That was what she asked me.

Why? Why? Why?

"You do not want to take care of my grandchildren, do you"?

Her complaining went on and on every minute, every hour, and every day.

I told her, "I am so sorry. I will make sure I use starch and iron their clothes. I will make sure to try very hard to make them look neat and clean all the time."

I never thought about to argued back with her. I tried to be a good old fashion Japanese wife.

I only knew the way I had grown up. We learn to be patient and take the blame.

She said, "Do not argue with me. I know you did not iron or did not use starch. They look sloppy. My grandchildren deserve to have the best. They should have expensive designer clothes all the time with her furious face. No matter how much I tried to give children very good, clean expensive dresses, she wasn't satisfied.

For every move the kids made, I would receive complain from Linda. Every single day

she made sure to remind me how useless I was, over and over. Linda complaining about children's clothes and their behavior just gave her another reason to scold me.

when I was growing up in Japan, my mother used to say to me, "Don't buy any cheap items. When you buy cheap stuff you think you got a bargain but it will lose value or wear out quickly. You will get tired of the item very soon. Expensive stuff lasts longer. In the end you will save money."

I remembered that and since then, I never

bought cheap items for myself or anybody else. Usually I did not buy anything if I did not have enough money.

I gave Bob's children the best clothes and made sure they were clean all the time, but Linda was never happy.

Linda said, "Kazuko does not want to spend money, and she buys cheap children's clothes! You know she is a Japanese and stupid. She doesn't know how to take care of the children and her husband."

Some of my neighbors told me what Linda said to them, "my poor son and grandkids!"

Linda wore a mask of a good, caring grandmother's face. She was a super talented actress! I could not believe.

When Linda started to speak to me she always yelled at me. Maybe she forgot to speak kindly and softly to me.

Her mind was already made up, that I was a loser and not a good wife.

She took away my pride and dignity very

successfully. I became a scared, no good, useless person.

She knew how to bring me down to the very lowest point and keep me there. She wouldn't allow me to get up from the lowest place.

When I was at my lowest point, she said to me, "That is where you belong. You should stay there. You should not think you are a better person because you are nothing."

She always told me. "Because of you your husband drink you should stop him. You are too stupid and useless that is why he does not want to come home on time. He doesn't' want to look at you. You are an eye sore."

I always said to her "I am so sorry. I don't know why he won't come home. I don't know why he drinks too much. I will try harder to make him come home and stop drinking. I'm so sorry. Everything is my fault."

That was the way Japanese were. I honored her and I respected her. I never thought about arguing with her.

Finally I started to believe maybe this was my fault. Maybe I didn't take good care of Bob and his children.

Was that the reason my husband wouldn't come home on time? Was the children's bad behavior because of me?

Was I a lousy stepmother? Was I a lousy wife? Was I useless? Was everything my fault like his mother said?

What happened to me? Where was my pride and strength? Where was my stubbornness?

Where was my confidence? Where were they? Where did they go? I thought people never changed. But I changed.

I knew in my heart. I did everything. I tried very hard to please them. After I came to this country, I never took a day or an hour or a minute off to rest myself.

I was not allowed to become sick. I was not allowed to stay in bed. I was a working machine. I was a robot. I was not able to have any feelings about what I wanted to do or what I did not want to do. I worked hard for them but they said my work was not good enough.

Linda said to me, "Bob and his children hate you. Nobody likes you. You should go back where you came from." She reminded me all the time.

I felt his mother's hate everywhere. I did not realize how words could be so powerful.

It made me to started thinking again, maybe I could not do right, because I was or I did not know American way? Was I stupid and useless? I started to believe his mother was right. That was so painful. If I lost my pride and dignity, I was nothing.

I used to be a very strong stubborn woman, like a stone head. I had a lot of energy and was a workaholic.

I own a very successful custom made dress shop and I was a well known designer in Japan. Now I felt like a lost child. I did not know what to do.

As I explained before, Nancy was stealing and lying. She yelled at me bite my arm and kicking me every day.

When I caught her stealing, I grabbed her hand and took my jewelry away from her.

She started biting my arm, kicking me and punching me.

I asked her to stop and I told her, “You have to stop stealing from me.”

She could punch me and kick me, but I couldn’t touch her. Even when I combed her hair, I had to be very careful, because She told her grandmother I was hurting her.

Linda said to me in an angry voice with a furious face. “You are not to discipline my grandchildren. These children are not yours. Do not even lay one finger on them. I know you make excuses to try to hurt my grandkids. You cannot spank them. If you spank my grandchildren, I will take your son away from you, and I will report you to the authorities. I will make sure they send you back to Japan without your son. I do not want to hear any complaints from Nancy. Do you understand me?"Her face was so hateful.

When I complained to Nancy, I got a call from Linda. "You should not punish her. She does not do anything wrong. You just hate her because she is not your kid. You will not touch her or scold her." I could not reason with Nancy. Nancy knew I could not spank her.

Nancy said to me "What are you going to do? Are you going to hit me?" She yelling and stuck her face toward me.

I said, "I never hit you. Why do you say that? You have to stop lying and stealing from me or any other person." She did not answer. She never stopped stealing or lying. She kept stealing from me until everything Was gone. I did not understand why.

How could she act that evil way?

She liked to bring anything of mine from the house to school.

Many times I asked her to stop, but she never listened. Each time I asked her to stop stealing, she started to laugh at me and fighting and kicking me. She was so hateful.

One evening I told my husband, "Nancy is taking my stuff from the house and bringing it to school. I am losing my memories from Japan. I am not able to replace the items which I've lost. Would you please tell her not take anymore?"

He said to me; with very agitate face, "I've heard from my mother that you are making up many stories saying that my children's behavior is bad. They wouldn't do such things. You should stop making up stories and telling me my children are bad."

I was shocked! I knew him once, as a sweet, thoughtful, kind man, who used to trust me and care about me. Had that man disappeared? What had happened to him? Where had he gone? Where was he? Where could I find the same man I married in Japan? He had changed.

Now I knew my husband would not believe me. He refused to believe me. I understood he did not want to make waves with his mother. But I needed his trust and support.

I said to myself, “I am your wife, I need you, where are you?”

I wished he would listen to me and help me. I did not have anybody to talk to. I was left alone in this big strange county.

Nancy spoke to me like a demented person with a hateful voice. She just laughed at me.

It didn’t matter what kind of items they were. She showed them to her friends and laughed at me or trashed my things. She told her friends, how stupid I was. She succeeded in hurting me deeply.

Some kid's mother brought back some Japanese items of mine to me, and She said," I feel very sorry for you."

One morning; I came out from my bathroom and saw Nancy trying to choke my son. He was not a year old yet. When I saw her, I acted without thinking. I pulled her hair to get her away from my son.

When I pulled her away from my son, Nancy started kicking and punching me, and then she stormed out of the house.

I cannot remember what I said to her or what I did also I did not know where she went. I only remembered that a policeman entered my house to arrest me.

When the policeman found me, I was holding my son, covering him with my whole my body to protect him so no one could hurt him.

I was sitting on the edge of my bed, and I was shaking. My shaking would not stop. I watched the policeman's face with empty feeling eyes and my mouth opened and close like a golden fish, in the tank, because I wanted to say something, but no words came out of my mouth.

My face was blank and exhausted. I was like a dead tree any soft wind blow; it would break down to ground.

My tears were dripping down to my son's face. I was surprised I still had the energy to cry.

The policeman told me, that he was going to arrest me and take my son away from me for my son's protection.

I do not understand why? I wished he will explained me what I did wrong and wished I could explain to him what really happen.

I wish he would listen to me. My son was the only thing making me survive. If I lost him I would probably die. Didn't you know my son meant more than my life? How could I hurt him? I would not hurt my son.

I tried scream but my word never came out.

I tried to explain, with my tears and I held my son very tight, so the policeman couldn't take him away from me. It looked like I was hiding my son inside of my body.

The policeman told me he would call welfare for child protection and they would take my son away, and he would report to authority, so they would send me back to Japan without my son, with very loud voice.

He stormed out of my house with very an angry face in a very violent way. He slammed my door so hard, I could still hear the sound of the door shut.

My son and I were left alone in my house. I was still shaking. I was so scared and so afraid to lose him but the policeman did not come back and I never hear from welfare or policeman. I realized what was happening to me then. I had to watch my son more carefully, when Bob's family was around.

I had to keep him very close to me at all times. Even at night, I couldn't let him sleep in the baby crib alone. I became like a watch dog. I paid attention to any noise.

When I could hear their footsteps or any tiny noise, I jumped out even in the middle of the night.

My eyes were wide open, and I was ready to protect my son anytime he needed me.

When I married I gave my life to my husband. I should work hard for him and not complain. I should have no personal feelings or my own selfish desires. "I should, I could, I want, I need," these words were not in my dictionary. I should try hard to please him, especially Linda.

I treated Linda better than I treated my own mother. If I tried harder, someday the sun would shine, and a sunny day would come. I hope. No matter how difficult or how badly have been treated, I should obey.

More badly I was treated I should work harder. I tried as hard as I could.

I had treated his mother like the most

important person in the whole world. I must try harder to please her. That is being, "a good wife" in Japan.

I gave all my life to them, and I tried as hard and as much, as I could. But still Linda said to me, "You are not good enough."

I became exhausted, and I had lost all my energy. I couldn't work for them anymore.

I had used myself up and nothing was left in me. I started to question myself again.

Maybe I was weak and did not work hard enough? Maybe, Maybe, But now I lost.

The first time I arrived in this country, I had a lot of respect for Bob and his family. Now I did not have any feelings for them. I just worked hard, without feeling.

This was my duty. I knew that, but I became so weak. I could not obey her any more. I knew I had to, but I couldn't. I couldn't respect them, and I couldn't honor them. Everything I did was wrong. I was a big failure.

I had done everything. I had worked very hard, that I thought. I knew I should try harder than now, but my body was shutting down. I couldn't eat. I couldn't sleep.
I couldn't think. I really believed dying would be better and easier. If I stayed here, I would probably take my own life. Dying was easier to me than staying with his family.

I wished I could die right now. I wished I could forget everything. Just go to sleep and be reborn to a different level, a different life. Maybe it would be a better life.

But If I died, what would happen to my son? That was not fair to him. He had not asked to be born. It was my duty to make sure my son would grow up to have his own life. Until then I had to be strong.

I knew that but I did not have energy left in myself to please Bob's family anymore.

The most concerned was I was a big failure. We Japanese can't fail. Failing was a disgrace to my family.

I couldn't fail, but I did not know how I could please them, especially his mother.

I tried everything so hard to please her but it was never good enough.

I started to think again, was I a failure? Wasn't I good enough for them? Didn't I try harder? Maybe I had not tried hard enough. Maybe everything that had happened was my fault?

Maybe I did not know how to take care of my husband and his family? Maybe my Japanese way of thinking was wrong? Maybe my husband's mother was right. Was I dummy and stupid Japanese?

I was surprised I started thinking that everything was my fault.

I thought I had tried everything, even though I did not have enough sleep. I was always working for them from early in the morning until late at night. Wasn't this good enough? What more did they want from me.

The path I took was not always the path I

wanted to take, but there I was. It was a hard life and a wrong life. My choice was wrong. I believed if I tried hard, some day they would understand me.

Linda wore human masks on her face in front of my husband or in front of strangers. She took it off when they were gone.

I believed she came from hell and she would take me down to hell.

I realized she was an evil witch. I think she put spell on me to make me miserable. I didn't complain, I gave them whatever I could but this was not good enough for them. I did not know what more I could do. My mind was shutdown. I was exhausted, and my body had nothing left at all. I did not feel anymore. I was skinny my weight was under 80 pounds. I couldn't' eat. I couldn't sleep. I was walking like a zombie. I had no feelings, no tears left to cry. Inside of me there was nothing left at all.

One day I washed and cleaned up my son

put him in clean clothes, and I got a few baby clothes, some diapers and put them in a diaper bag.

I looked up a taxi's telephone number from phone book, and I wrote it down very hard on the paper pad.

I called the taxi. The taxi company had trouble understanding me on the phone, but somehow we connected, and the taxi came to my house a few minutes later.

I picked up the top piece of paper that had the taxi company's telephone Number.

I did not want to leave any information and I did not want them to know where and how I left the house.

I did not know that when I wrote the number, I pressed down so hard on the pad of paper the number soaked down to the paper underneath. (I found out This later).

I was so nervous my heart was pumping so fast that it seemed like it would stop.

I picked up my son, and I held him as tight

as I could. In my other hand I carried his diaper bag.

I got into the taxi and asked him to take me to any motel.

My blood pressure was jumped up and down. My mind was occupied. I was so nervous, and my heart was beating very fast. I felt the taxi was going too slowly. It seemed like nothing was moving.

I told him to go faster and faster. I was impatient. I was afraid somebody would spot me, and he or she would take me out of the tax and bring me back to that horror house.

I only wanted to get out this horrible trailer park.

It took a few minute to get out the park but it seem like forever to me.

Finally we were out of the trailer park. What a relief!

When we were far from the park and as the taxi went further I felt a little better.

The taxi driver took us to a small motel.

It looked very clean. It seemed like a good safe neighborhood.

I think that the taxi driver sensed something about me while I was in the taxi, I realized.

He never asked me any questions after we had a few short conversations. He had found out I couldn't speak English well.

He watched me through the mirror and his mind told him "Poor lady. She does not understand English well. She looks exhausted. She is too skinny, like a skeleton. She looks like she has had no food for too long time. She called the taxi to take her to some motel with her baby. Doesn't she have any place to go? Something must have happened to her. She must need help."

I thought he tried to help me. That was why he took me to a better motel in a neighborhood where I would be safe.

When the taxi reached its destination, the driver got out. He went to the office and got a key for me while I waited inside the taxi for the driver to come back.

I was so scared that my body would not stop shaking. The taxi driver came back and gave me a key.

He said good luck to me with his warm smile? I thought.

I did not understand his English very well. How could I understand him when he spoke English with a strange accent? But I felt warmth and kindness from him.

I thanked him, and I got out of the taxi. Then the taxi left.

While I was walking into the motel, I felt his warmth. Warmth started wrapping itself around me, and I felt a little relief. I still believed that he had tried to help me in his way.

After the taxi left, all of sudden I started to get scared. In the taxi I had some kind of protection from the driver. Now nobody would protect me.

I ran into the room quickly and locked the door.

I started changing my son's diaper. I tried to calm myself down for my son. He had had a long exciting day. He did not need that. He needed to feel safe and happy.

I started singing Japanese songs to him. I did not know if he understood our situation or not.

He tried to open his mouth, and he tried to clap hands with me, and he smiled at me. He was such an innocent and wonderful baby!

While I was watching my baby and playing with him all of the sudden I felt hungry. I started running hot water in the bathroom sink. I put his formula in the sink to warm up his bottle. The milk temperature began getting warm.

I put a few drops of milk on my wrist to found out if it was the right temperature. I started feeding my son first.

The innocent baby drank the milk without any fear. He seemed trusting me and very happy. He acted like nothing had happen to us. I had been afraid of running away from our home to a strange place. He was laughing!

After I finished feeding my baby, I started to eat a piece of bread. That was all I could take with me when I left the house.

I felt that bread tasted so wonderful, better than any other meal I could compare.

For the first time I was not afraid to eat. I did not worry about hearing my mother-in-law say, "You eat too much or too slow," with her furious face. She always told me, "You take too much time to eat. Who do you think you are? Hurry up, finish and start working."

I could not hear her voice now. I could take as much as I wanted, and I could taste the food. I could enjoy it. This was heaven.

My son and I did not have enough food to

eat or enough money. There were only few dollars left, but I was relieved.

I sat and thought about all the reason why I had no money.

When my mother's (from Japan) money came to my house, Bob's whole family came to my house. His mother, sister and brother got together and tried to take my money away from me. They were like vultures.

Somehow I had managed to save some money. There was only a little left for us but we were free.

We did not have to be afraid anymore. I was safe and free now. I did not fear for his life at this moment. This was the first time I felt safe. What a relief! It was good to not worry about my son's life.

For so long a time I had not had any good sleep. I had never had this peaceful feeling. Quiet air blew so softly it wrapped around me and touched me and held me so gently, telling me everything was going to be all right

The breeze told me "You are safe now. You should enjoy this moment of peace and quiet. Go to sleep and enjoy it." It sounded like a lullaby to me I finally fell asleep on the bed, my son sleeping next to me.

The sound of the wind was telling me go To sleep, and a bird was singing giving me a moment of peace. This peaceful and quiet moment made me fall into a deep sleep.

I prayed, "Please do not take away this peace, safety and the sanctuary of sleep." But evil was not releasing me.

I don't know how long I slept before I heard some noise.

This noise started to disturb me very much. It took my peace away, and I woke up.

"Was somebody knocking on my door? Was I sleeping? Was I dreaming? Who were they to wake me up and break my peace? They had no right to break my peace and knock at my door! Why don't they leave me alone? Go away."

Is it true? Was somebody outside my door? Who could it be? It no one knew where I was.

All of a sudden, goose pimples appeared and my whole body started shaking.

I peeked out the window, and saw a few police cars. A few policemen and a few people stood outside of my door.

I recognized my husband's mother, his sister's, and his children standing outside my door.

I could not imagine how they found me. Nobody could have known where I was.

A few policemen were outside of my room. Somebody knocked on my door.

I started to be scared I started shaking. I felt ice cold water run though my spine.

I put blankets all over me and tried to Hide from them, but my shaking would not stop.

I started to panic, "What should I do. I did not do anything wrong. I was not a criminal.

Why were policemen out there? Why were policemen outside of my room? Would they hurt me? Would they take my son away?

Why? Why? Why.

I started moving a few chairs against the door. I would not open this door. I did not want to open this door. I have to try to stop this door from opening. I couldn't let them open my door.

I would like to escape from here with my son if I could. But where could I go? How could I run away from here? What could I do?

I heard a familiar voice calling my name.

"Kazuko, would you open the door? I am very worried about you. You do not know America, and you cannot speak English well. Here in America people will hurt you. It is Very dangerous. You will be hurt. Please open the door and come home with us before you get hurt. I can't leave you and your baby here alone." It was Linda saying.

"It is very dangerous to stay here. You should come home with us. We are very concerned for you and your baby." Bob's sister said. "We care about you very much."

"Lie. Lie. Lie. Why did they lie? Why wouldn't they leave me alone? "I said to myself.

"We are worried about you. You should open the door and let us come in so we can take you home with us. Otherwise we will have to send you back to Japan without your son." Linda said.

"Please open the door." They repeated over and over.

The sound was very soft and care. It was strange to hear their voices so calm and gentle. I had never heard that before. The policeman would believe them! I didn't know what they had said to the policeman. I didn't' know what I should do or think. Think! Think and think. I walked around in the room up and down. I tried to think. I knew I positively must not open this door. I'd never open the door! No matter what, I wouldn't open this door. I couldn't and I shouldn't open this door I would not go home with them. I'd rather die here.

I had to think what should I do? Panic! I had used up all my energy. Nothing was left in me. I had no energy to think. I didn't know what I should do. I knew I had to think before the door opened.

I did not want to go home with them. Neither did I want to go home to Japan without my son.

I walked around the room like a bear in the zoo, back and forth with a lot of fear.

This did not make any sense at all. Why can they take my baby away? Why policeman listen to them instead find out what really happen? Where I stand and was I right to explain and get help? I did not understand American way.

I thought this was wrong but I did not

want to argue with them cause to lose my son either. What should I do? Should I listen to them? Should I kill myself before open this door like brave worrier in Japan?

Bob's mother always told me that the United State could take a baby away from a mother and just send only the mother back to where she had come from. It was scary. I did not know what to do.

I wished I was smart. So I would know what to do. I said to myself over and over. "I do not want to go home."

While I was thinking, I heard some sounds from the door.

Somebody was trying to open my door. Panic! I saw the key. The policeman was holding a key, and he was trying to open my door.

I tried to stop them from opening it. I tried to make a barricade pushing a table and chair against the door so they couldn't open it. That I thought,

"I will fight. I am determined. I won't let them open my door. I won't let them in my room. They must not open the door. They must not open this door. Please don't let them open my door please."

Somehow a policeman opened my door. He did not say a word. He looked at me with a very angry face.

He took out his handcuffs, and he put them on my hands.

I looked at him not understanding, I was numb and confused my body was paralyzed, but the policeman seemed like, he did not care what I thought or what I felt.

After he put cuffs on my hands, he pulled me out of the room in a very violent way.

He pushed me in the police car. He treated me as if I was not human. He made me terrified. That Policeman took away my trust and made me hated policemen.

They should not treat me like that. Even though I did not know much about America,

I thought it was wrong.

I did not know what his mother said to the policemen. Maybe they thought I was a monster, and they had to keep me in the cage? But why?

What did I do wrong? Why do you treat me this way?

I thought something was wrong with this treatment then I realized that what I thought was not important to them at all. If I tried to fight, they would have more excuse to hate me. They would take my son away from me, and I would never have a chance to see him again. I knew this was my only chance to against them. But I had failed again.

Why didn't they understand me? "Please take me to some other place better than that horror house. Even jail is better than going home.

"Please do not take me home," I begged the policeman. "Please put me in jail instead of sending me home.

I must not go home. I don't want to go home."

I repeated this many times to the policeman, but my wish was not granted.

They took me home to my trailer against my wishes.

When I got out of the police car, I was humiliated.

At my trailer, people were crowded Around looking at me just like I was a bank robber or a killer.

Some people were watching me with very confused faces. Some seemed to have mixed emotions.

I was home. I was in the horror house again!

Well, for just a very little time I had felt free, and I had felt I was alive, but my dream was broken.

My dream was broken by my mother-in-law and my sister-in-law.

Thank you very much for your resentment and despising me!

Why wouldn't you leave me alone?

Why do you hate me so much?

I did not do anything to make you hate me.

I had a very short time of adventure but my adventure was over now.

IN JAPAN

I was born to a Samurai family and raised in the old fashioned strict Japanese system. Ancient Japanese blood was running through my body, but I tried to live the new wave of Japan. I was caught between two different cultures.

People tough, I was typical young, full energy, obnoxious and a lot of mischievous spoiled rotten girl.

Maybe it was true or maybe not. Some part of me seemed like an obnoxious spoiled child. Really I was a shy and in secure person, and I did not know how to socialize with others. I was scared to talk to people. But I pretended (I was not shy, and I had confidence in myself) very well.

Japanese Summer is hot and sticky and uncomfortable.

When I sat in a chair, my sweat run down from my face and it ran a competition every day and every minute on my face. When I sat on a chair, in five minutes my clothes were soaked.

Here in Japan, when we walked outside on the street, people are everywhere. Shoulder to shoulder they bumped each other. People are crammed in here in Japan. Too many people make it hotter than it was.

Even in the extremely heat, we still dress up all the time in long skirts and long sleeve shirts. Sometime we were allowed to wearing short sleeved shirts.

The dresses must be starched and ironed. We did not allow wearing tank tops and short pants when I grew up.

I always carried a fan in the summer. I never thought anything special about a Japanese fan, but now, as I think back, a fan is ethnic and original. Something about a fan has elegance and beauty.

In old time Japan, Samurai used the fan to communicate with each other specially, love from man to woman or woman to man.

Each used the fan as a signal to deliver her or his feelings to each other.

It is a very discreet way because a long, long time ago. To love somebody with your free will was prohibited. Duty come first love come last.

Hot summer afternoon, I could go up to the top of the department building to cool down.

Department stores were seven or eight floor high and top of the floor had tall fence around and the fence was curved inside to the building. Usually they had a bar and they playing Hawaiian music is one corner and other corner was play place *kingya sukui(catch gold fish in the small pool) pachinko(Japanese pin ball game), and many other play station* for family.

I sat in a chair listened Hawaiian music and sip cold drink. I let the wind played though my hair with nice soft breezing and cooled me dawn It was wonderful and relaxing.

Also another way I could go to a restaurant to get cooled down.

Japan's underground shopping malls are huge it looks like whole town fit into the shopping mall. I felt the whole town is there. Stream is run from first floor(B1) to second(B2) and third floor(B3), there are many goldfish swim through in the stream, some people were throw some coin into the water. Also air conditioners always give us just right comfortable temperature. Especially in summer time, I go to a special restaurant, it has very icy cold water with cold noodles running down from the top of the hill though the bamboo pipe.

At the bottom of the hill people are waiting reaching for noodles. People can get noodles put in their own bowl to eat.

It cools people down and it's fun.

We have all kinds of ways to cool down during the hot summer.

Osaka was a little south of Japan and famous for food. All kinds' of restaurants were here, from French, Spanish, Russian, Chinese, and Korea. Many ethnic foods were here.

I had a small custom dress shop in Osaka Japan. The front room of my shop had a custom made table and a few custom made chairs. The customers could sit down comfortable and enjoyed rich taste of atmosphere.

A few sketch books and sample material books were on the table customers to see.

On the wall I had a few photos from my fashion show. I enlarged them, and hung them on the wall.

In the back room of the store, I had eight sewing machines. They kept working from morning to late evening.

I had another room. It had three walls mirrors for the customer for fitting. This room was my working place. The thick lavender color carpet lay on the floor. Always soft French music added to our shop's atmosphere. It was a very simple but richly tasted room.

When I started this store I was in the university's second year. I tried to do something besides study. It had taken off well. I was 20 years old, full dreams with a lot of curiosity girl. I was dreaming all the time. People called me a strange girl, but I had confidence in my work, I thought I was a normal.

I did not like to socialize with others. I did

not have in me any special conversation or nice things to say to other people. Always my words came out wrong way. I would say something I did not mean to offend people without realizing.

I did not have any special friends to hang out with to drink or chase boys.

Other people called me “a boring girl” but I did not realize I was boring.

I worked very hard. Most of my sleep time was in the train or in the bus. I usually stayed up until two or three o’clock in the morning. When I got up it was six o’clock same day in the morning. I had only a few hours sleep a day.

If I was exhausted, or after my deadline (my fashion show) was over, sometime I slept to the afternoon. When I started my own business, my sleeping habits were Changed. Before I started my business, I used to go to bed at 9:00 pm, and, no matter how much I tried I couldn’t stay up late

My mother used to tell me, “Why don’t you stay up and socialize with your cousin or aunt. They traveled so far to get here to see you. ”

I told my mother, “It’s time to go to bed. I can’t stay up. I have to go to sleep.”

Kicking my feet bounce up and down like a little spoiled kid nagging to the mother.

I made a bed and then I went to sleep. I did not think about other people at that time.

In Japan the bedroom and living room are the same, (Day time we put bed away and night time we made bed in the living room). So I tried to make my bed in the living room. (My mother’s house had two living room. one is a Japanese style and other is a European style). We prefer Japanese style living room In which it’s usually the custom to sit and have a good time with my family.

I did not care if company was in my house

or not. I had to go to bed at 9.00 pm on the dot, like an alarm clock. There for my mother's guest have to move one living room to other room.

I missed too many parties while I was in school. Many school friends told me, "You are not fun. How can you go to sleep so early?"

I thought why couldn't I have interest in going to a party like my friends do? I always felt lonely. When I thought I had to socialize with other people, goose pimples showed up all my body and I felt sick.

I did not have confidence in myself to associate with another people, so I told myself, "why am I spending my precious time just getting together to sit around and drink (we usually drink a pot of Japanese tea)? Have stupid conversation is a waste my time! Why do I have to waste my precious time? I am not interested in throwing away my valuable times."

I don't know why I feel like that. Was I obnoxious? Was I crazy?

People thought, I was weird, but I thought I was perfect, and I was a normal girl. Maybe other people were weird, but deep inside me, I always felt inferior.

I thought everybody did not like me. I was isolated from other students for a long time. But other hand when I got know people I was a crown and made people laugh. I love to see people laugh. I tried to remind myself how lucky I was.

I had my own fashion show, twice a year. Also I had many good customers who wanted the top line fashions and spent a lot of money for their clothes.

When my fashion shows were near, it was a murder. I had to decide what kind of material to use, and what color for that season. What kind style there was going to be long skirt or a short skirt? What kind of neck line and collar or what kind of shoulder line. I have to come up with many design with new material, and I have to special order my material from the fabric company for every season.

I have to interview many models. (I did not own any model, so I had to go to an agency to hire a few models.)

A book keeper and eight stitches worked for me. Theses stitches were excellent at sewing. Also there was an illustrator and me. I could sew a little bit, but not for the business.

My job was fitting (temporally saw a dress on the customer before finishing the dress) to the customer and taking order.

It was a busy shop. A few of my designs were published in a fashion books few times.

I lost my sleep many times when my special deadlines for my fashion show came near. It was a very exciting business I loved it and I lived it.

I did not need any of my time to look for fun. I believed. I already had a good time with my business. I thought who needs a fun. That was a trash. I never went to any parties even though I had many chances'. Parties were wasted time to me.

I had to do so many things, and I did not have any extra time for so called "good times." I enjoyed what I was doing.

If I had the time to go to a party I would rather sleep in. I wore old pajamas and getting in the kotatu to watch television and eat my kind of food.

When I was alone, I didn't have to worry about other people's eyes or their feeling. I didn't worry about what to say to other people, or if I talked very stupidly.

I always made stupid conversation.
That's why I liked to be alone. Because I could say what I want, or whatever I please. I felt free.

It sounded nice, but I thought I was afraid

of people's opinions. So I just kept try busy and made sure I did not go to any parties.

Late one morning, my good customer (nayoko) came to my shop. She told me,

"My Company where I work is going to have a very big party next month. I wish you would come to our party. I would like to introduce you to many of my coworkers and my boss's wife (Hediko).

Hediko loves beautiful dresses and your imagination is terrific. I know Hediko will love your dresses and I love your designs too. Please come, even few hours of your time would be a nice." She showed me she was excited.

I thought "Oh my god! I have to go to her party? "Panic what can I do?" I had to finding some good excuse so I don't have to go to the party. I couldn't find any. Why couldn't I find any excuse?

Oh well I just keep my answer simple, "I will think about it, and I will let you know."

With an obnoxious manner, of courses I never thought to attend it.

Few days after Nayoko called me again and asked me whether or not I was coming to her company's party.

I told her, "I would like to come to your Part, but I am so busy that a few hours of my time is too much to lose. Sorry I will not be able to come to your party." I used a very stern voice and acted cheekily.

Because of my shyness, I couldn't handle her in a normal way. I acted as if I was a very snob and I treated her badly. But I did not mean to treat her that badly.

I thought, she thinks about me "I am an obnoxious woman, and wonders why nobody likes me."

She said to me, "I understand you are busy woman. You just show up and whenever you have to leave, you can leave. You do not need to stay long. Just come."

I was terrified to go to her party. But I

couldn't find any good excuse. I was look for excuse since I heard first invitation. I thought, I control my life well, but true was complete opposite. I was wimp and scared shy a little girl.

Do I have to go to her party? Well what could I do? I couldn't say no to her (my wimp and shyness). Well I just go her party with fear, because I did not want to hurt her feeling, that was why I agreed to attended her company's party.

When I thought about it I became very depressed. I prayed and hoped it would be canceled.

I hired a taxi to get the party. It took place at the Hilton hotel.

It was a lavish party but not huge. Many people wore kimonos. Some people wore evening gowns. I wore simple princess style of dress.

My friend Nayoko saw me when I arrived to the hotel. As soon as she saw me she ran to me with an anxious face. Her face told me, she couldn't wait to tell me something.

She said to me "I would like to introduce you to a very good friend of mine." Middles of her explain she pulled my hand and dragged me to her friend.

She said, "His name is Bob. He is an American. An American company sent him to our company as an engineer and problem solver. He has been staying in Japan for about ten years. While he was staying in Japan he went back home to U.S.A. few times. My company wants him to stay in Japan and work for us for good. He is a hard worker and a very kind hearted man."

I smiled at him as greeting, but I never wanted to make any conversation with him.

I did not want to become friends. I did not want to know him at all. I tried keeping my mind busy. If I kept thinking about my business, I would not scare people and make me confident. It safe that way.

Bob spoke to me, but I did not hear any words he said. I did not interest. I walked from him middle of he was talking.

Suddenly my exhaustion attacked me. I felt so weak and so tired. I had to sit down some hidden place to relax.

I looked for some place to sit down. I finally found a chair in the corner. This chair was situated much hidden from everybody.

I thought nobody would see me. I sat down in the chair. As soon as I sat down, I fell asleep.

My sleep was more important than this party. How weird was I. I couldn't even enjoy this party! I did not want to know how other people thought about me or other people's opinions.

I did not want to find out because I was afraid of what people thought about me.

Just sleep and keep quiet, the time will pass. Hope. I did not feel fear if I was sleeping.

When I woke up, a few people were

staring at me. They surrounded me and looked at me in a very strange way. They made me feel guilty.

Had I done something very bad? They made me uncomfortable.

I was so humiliated and embarrassed. A fire run through my body.

Hope I didn't have to see any more of these people again. I covered my face and rushed out of the door.
I wanted to fly out of this hotel.

I went home without saying goodbye to my friend. I was so embarrassed how could I face her!

A few days passed, and then I got a telephone call. It was my friend Nayoko.

She said to me, "Thank you for coming to my company's party. I am so sorry, I missed you, and I would like to make it up. I would like to have a dinner with you. Please, would you join me?"

Is she not mad at me for what I did to her

at her party? I embarrassed you and your company. You still wanted me?

In Japan destroying somebody's face is not forgiven, but you forgave me? You had such a big heart, that I thought.

My embarrassment and my shameful feeling made me to say "Thank you but no thank you. "My voice was full of awkwardness

I had embarrassed her enough. I did not want to embarrass her anymore, I thought.

I told her "I do not have time, because my Show is in the very near future and I was very busy."

She asked my schedule with a very calmly voice.

I felt shame what I did to her company's party, also I had an obligation to her. Besides I love to eat. She got me there by my weakness.

Eating good food was my pleasure. How could I refuse? But I rather go to restaurants by myself instead of with a friend. I always went to restaurants alone. That way it was very comfortable for me to what or how much I eat.

But I felt, I owed her deeply. I agreed to meet her at a restaurant near my shop. This place had a very good noodle store. The food was excellent but not expensive restaurant.

It was not fancy, just quick food like McDonald, In the United States.

My hair was a mess and my clothes were not fashionable even though my business was a fashion business. I was tiny and any clothe would fit me well. That was what I thought. What an arrogant!

I usually kept a few clothes at my shop for emergencies. They were very simple regular clothes. I wore a nice light purple with shade of gray color princess style dress with no sleeves. I looked into a mirror and I told myself what a beautiful dress I wore. This dress was very simple, but had a very rich.

This dress made me, a very elegant and beautiful woman! I was so arrogant wasn't I?

Like I said, I was much too snobbish woman. Maybe so call pride?

While I was walking to the restaurant my feeling was like, there was a very dark cloud hanging over my head.

My feet were so heavy, like a ball of chain tie around my feet and tided me down to ground and did not go forward.

I tried to walk faster but I felt it was too far to get to the restaurant. I would like to run back to my shop and hide. Hope I do not have to go to the restaurant.

While I walked with thinking try to running back to my shop I already reached to the restaurant. But I did not have courage to going inside. I stood a while outside of the restaurant.

I took a big breath. I tried to get myself a little brave and told myself, like mother tell a little kid to make her understand. You do not scare. You have to going there. I know I do not want to, but I have to.

I kept saying myself and tried to give myself for a little push. Finally I find a little courage lead me go inside to the restaurant.

There were my friend and Bob waiting for my arrival.

We sat in the corner and we talked, we ate, we talked and we laughed. I realized I was not nervous at all.

We stayed in the restaurant quite a long time. As matter of fact, I realized, I needed to just relax and have dinner with a good friend, this experience was so nice for me. I felt little relief and escape from busy and pressure living, I felt very good. I realized I was rejuvenated.

A few hours passed. I returned to the rat race of business again.

It was busy and busies no time to think anything. No time to eat or do anything except business

One afternoon Bob showed up at my shop.

I was surprise! How did he get this address? I wondered. We usually did not give any information about other people without person's permission.

Maybe my friend gave it to him? But she shouldn't. Then I realized I had my business and very easy to find me where my shop was.

He saw me I was busy. He looked around my shop very carefully, like a detective trying to find some criminal evidence.

He was looking for something to do. Nobody talked to him. I did not have any time and I did not want to talk to him ether. I hoped. "Go away!"

He stayed only a few minute and he left. What a relief!

After my fashion show was over, I invited my good customers to the loyal hotel which was my favorite hotel. Bob and Nayoko were there I was surprised because I did not invite

Bob. I never paid any attention to him or Nayoko either.

I knew Bob and Nayoko were always together. They were inseparable. But I felt he should not be here. Why was he here? But I did not have the courage to ask him, so I just shut my mouth and kept quiet.

I kept myself busy this way I felt very comfortable and safe. I was afraid of people. I think better to not talk them at all.

I loved to be busy and I loved my business Let my coworker handle all my functions there for I did not need any social skills. That I thought. I did not missing anything important in my life, and I was doing very well for my age and for being a woman and I felt great!

Old Japan was a very hard country to live in for everybody, especially for a woman. Japanese society gives everybody a lot of pressure.

When we do anything, we have to be

perfect. We have to be number one and people expected excellent work. Any mistakes are not accepted. But it was very honest and trusted country.

For example, our verbal agreement was good as gold and you could believe verbal agreement and trusted. We did not take it back, or make excuses once we promised. Everybody keep their promises, no matter how hard was. We had to keep our promised with pride. We were tried harder even today.

A mistake is a shameful thing. Therefore, people always must do their job the best.

Beginning in 1969 International EXPO 70, started to be set up from each company.

My friend Hiromi asked me to help her company to set up for the Expo. Even though, I was busy I promised her I would help her.

The EXPO was started in September 1970. Before that time I was helping Hiromi. Bob was there helping his company. I was surprised to see him.

He started talking to me. Each time he tried I found some excuse to walk away.

I was very good to walking away from him, but he was stubborn man.

He kept trying to have some conversation with me any chance he had. That annoyed me.

Meanwhile, Bob and Hiromi became good friends. One day, Hiromi said to me she would like to have lunch with Bob and I .

I question myself did I have to have lunch with you and Bob? That made me nervures and scare.

I thought Bob's idea made hiromi to ask me to go lunch with them. I thought what a sneaky guy! He knew I couldn't say no to my friend.

We went to a restaurant in the expo pavilion. While in the restaurant, at the beginning, I was very quiet and I didn't join their conversation and felt separated and alone that was good and I was comfortable. Then they started to focus on me. My friend translated his many questions to me. His questions force me to have conversation and I felt I had to join their conversation I like or not. When I started to answer his question, I realized my shyness goes away. I could be myself. I didn't have to pretend anymore and felt I was relief.

I felt, they acting playful. Bob seem to be having so many questions about me! But he made me comfortable to talk to him.

After we had lunch at the EXPO, he started to come to my shop quite often.

I become little easy to hear his English, and I understand English a little bit more.

I was surprised myself laughing and talking to him. I realized. He was a sweet and very kind human being. He had reputation of hard worker with a sharp mind.

I talked to him in Japanese-English and he answered me back in English. I understood what he said and he understood what I said.

I was surprised myself in my English. I thought my English was good! I thought how smart I was I could talk in English to him even though I did not take an English course. It was Awesome!

It never occurred to me he could speak Japanese! My thought was he did not understand Japanese because he traveled always with his translator Nayoko.

As matter of fact I found out later, he could speak a few other languages too.

When I gradually got know him better. I discovered him an honest and caring person. Also he had humor and a very good personality with kind heart.

He made me laugh. I could respect somebody like him. I felt very fortunate. It was nice to meet someone I could trust.

It was nice to know some American's have decency, because many American service men here are terrible. They rape women and rape our country. They steal goods from stores and their behavior were very violent and go wild here.

I started to taking an English intensive course, not because of him, but because I needed English for the EXPO World Fair.

My English class probably had 25 to 30 students. Some students were preparing for the university exam. Some people were office workers hoping they would get better jobs. Some were business owners like me. Some were workers for foreign companies. It was a very unique class.

One day, my friend from English class asked me, whether People in our class go to see an American movie with Bob or not. They think that would be awesome.

I said to them, "I will asked Bob and I will give you an answer tomorrow in our class."

I asked Bob, "Our English class would like to go to movie with you. What do you think?" He said to me "I think that would be

Fun."

We met in the hotel lobby. Ten of us walk to a movie theater.

I felt like I was in school again and we were going on a kind of a field trip. We chose an American movie.

In Japan we have many American movie theaters also French, Chinese and other countries movie.

I do not remember name of the movie, but it was very unique story. The movie was about two soldiers, one from America, Lee Marvin and one from Japan, Mifune Toshiro.
They stuck somewhere on an island during the war. They were enemies. They swore at each other. They fought. They competed with each other. The Japanese soldier worked like an ant and created from rain water to drinking water.

As soon as the Japanese soldier went to bed the American soldier stole the precious water the Japanese soldier just had made.

The American soldier was an opportunist. He just sat up in the tree and watched the Japanese' hard work and laughed at him.

The American took any chance he had to steal from the Japanese.

Each time the Japanese lost the accumulation of his work; he swore to himself in Japanese and got angry.

When the American soldier saw the Japanese got angry he laughed at him.

Both talked two different languages and the two were fighting each other. Did they ever understand each other? I do not remember the end of the story.

While we watched the movie, when Bob laughed we were very quiet. During some parts of the movie, we laughed, but Bob was very quiet. Definitely we were different, but we had a good time in the movie theater.

After the movie, we went to a coffee house. Inside of the coffee house was European decor chairs were staffed and cover of leather. They were very comfortable. Coffee cups were custom made by famous artists and they were very expensive. In the background had very nice classic music was playing. It made us calm and relaxed

Usually Japanese coffee shops play classical music or French music.

A cup of coffee was around $10 and they did not refill coffee.

Many people just sat and listened to music. They forgot busy pressured times. They were enjoying a moment of peace.

Our group was trying to practice English on Bob. Bob was correcting their English very patiently at their request.

I started to notice a good side of Bob. At that time I did not know Bob could speak Japanese well.

I said to my group in front of Bob. "He is a funny face American. I thought American's had very beautiful faces and was attractive. I thought American people had blond hair with big blue eyes like a*lan doron* (this is a French mover star. I do not know how to spell correctly. He was a very popular in Japan), but Bob has a big nose instead big eyes and he is not my type at all." (This was an insult about Bob.) He was not handsome like a French movie star.

I pointed out with my Japanese language to my friends, what I didn't like about him.

I thought he won't be understood what I said to them. We laughed, but not Bob.

I felt how nice a man he was but I felt something about him make me did not want to associate. There for I try avoiding him as much as I could.

One afternoon Bob came to my shop and asked me to help his shopping. My feeling was "panic!" I had to help his shopping? Did I have to spend time with him? Even though, I was getting known about him a little better. Something about him annoyed me very much even though how nice man he was. I wished I could say no to him. I did not have the courage to say no to him or any other people. Oh well, I was a wimp. I was cowardice, and then I realized, he did help my English friend. Maybe he did not have a good friend to go shopping. In strange country he was alone, I felt sorry about him. In the end I agreed with his request.

We went to a department store. He bought a pearl necklace.

I never gave any thought of his shopping. I thought maybe he bought it for his mother.

I tried finding one that looks good but was not so expensive. Later I found out that jewelry was for my mother. If I had known I chosen different one, because I knew my mother's taste. Oh well.

At the same time he told me," I would like to invite your mother to a restaurant to have a dinner with us."

What a nerve! Don't you know by now?

Japanese women, especially my mother has nothing to do with American men? What a bold you are! You think I will have dinner with you too?"

I knew my mother wouldn't be joining us. But I did not tell him that, I just said to him, "I will ask." I thought I knew my mother's answer, but I did ask my mother anyhow.

My mother agreed to come to the restaurant.

I was surprised, because he was an American. What I heard from my mother just now I couldn't believe my ears. Was my mother all right? Maybe she did not hear me correctly. We would have dinner with an American man did she understand? Was she mentally all right? What was the matter with her? She would come to dinner with this American man? Don't I embarrass you enough?

I knew her from bottom of my heart. It was a shameful thing to have dinner with an

American man and me. She had a lot of courage to take action like this.

I admired her courage, but deep inside of me, I had hoped she would refuse this engagement.

The three of us had a dinner in a nice European style restaurant.

I saw Bob's face. His face was red like fire and his hands were shaking. He showed me he was very nervous.

It was a funny thing he never spoke Japanese to me while he was in Japan. I didn't know why. I never come to my mind, why he spoke to us English.

He asked me to tell my mother instead of speaking Japanese to her.

He told my mother he was so happy to meet me, he said how beautiful and how smart her daughter was." He told my mother many good things about me. I was little embarrassed to translate to her. Our dinner meeting went well. But my mother did not show me that she was proud of me, but I could tell how much she was proud of me.

Time passed by and Bob's appeared at my store quite often. I got used to seeing Bob. I thought about him what a smart and kind man.

Each appearance he left me with a nice feeling. Sometime his warmness made me calm and I could breathe.

Few days after, Bob came to my shop and asked me to marry him.

I never thought about marriage and I was not wife type. I was a business woman that was I thought.

I always had rebel about old fashion system. "This is a good a chance to tell my mother, her style is old fashion and I am a liberated woman. You can't keep me in an old fashion way."

I had fiancé since I was two years old. Of course this was my family and another family's decision. I never saw my future husband and I did not know what kind of a man he was.

Was he a handsome man or an ugly old baldheaded guy? I was in spite of my mother's decision. That was one reason to marry to Bob more than anything else. Another reason I would like to show my mother I could choose own my husband by myself.

Also, Bob was not bad looking even he was not my type, and he was not old like one hundred years old with no teeth bend back and half died really old guy.

I always believed that when I get married, my love would grow bigger and bigger and I would become a good wife "A proper wife." and I will make my family happier. I know the Japanese way.

I was a librated woman you know, when I was a child I told my mother, "I will find own my husband. I do not want to marry someone who I do not know. If I listen to you maybe he is one ugly old man with baldhead no teeth hundred years old and half dead man!"That was I told my mother.

If I think back now I was a pretty selfish, naïve and obnoxious woman. I thought I knew everything. I hated arrogant and obnoxious people. I did not realize I was that person then.

As soon as my mother heard my engaged announce her face showed me she was concern, but she did not say any word to me. Only I remember she told me, "I am always here for you, and I hope you made the right choice," Her dread voice with worried face.

I told my mother "even we marry we are going to stay in Japan. We are not moving away." But my mother showed me she was worry. Her sad voice and worried face stayed in the back of my head and stayed there like a picture had just been taken.

She tried very hard to be happy for me. Her mouth was shaking. She never complained

about how far I might move away or maybe we would never see each
other again. Maybe?

I arranged our marriage ceremony. I found the place we are going to have our ceremony.

This place used to be a Samurai's castle. It was an honor to have a marriage ceremony there. This place chooses customers and was not available to the public. I was excited to get the place. I arranged the food for our guests, also guests take present home (it had two layer of square middle size of boxes inside of boxes was made from all kind food that express happiness, wealth and long life. This is Japanese customers). I paid whole wedding expense. Also I hired few photographers.

Bob told me, "In the U.S.A. usually the man pays the expense, but I like Japan. Here women pay." He laughed. Truth was here Japan usually man pay whole wedding and future husband would give many gifts to new wife's parent (*yuinow)* it's show how value this woman have. Also how powerful future husband would be.

Gifts were extravagant. I did not want to be merchandise; I know I could pay my own expense. I never thought, it was his responsibility to pay for the wedding, but he insisted on paying some of the expenses. I told him not worry. I did not need your money I had plenty.

I needed to get away from the old fashioned style, and I would get new way of life. That was what I always thought.

The dress rehearsal was a night mare. I wore a traditional Japanese wedding gown (kimono), but not Bob. He wanted to wear traditional Japanese wedding kimono, but he was too tall and his arms were too long for Japanese kimono. His hands and feet were sticking out half way from the sleeves of the kimono and the Hakama (Japanese style of trousers) was too short for him, so we had to change his traditional Japanese clothes to an American style. Even those American styles of Clothes were still short in the pants and short in the sleeves of the tuxedo.

I had to order an especially made tuxedo. End up everything started to fit together like a puzzle.

We had a wedding ceremony in April of 1969. It was a wonderful time of the year, maybe the best season in Japan.

Many cherry blossoms were blooming all over. Wind blew so softly and blossoms petals were dancing around making small cycle to falling to the ground. Some were flying away to the sky. The Sun was smiling at me and flowers were starting open all over around me to bless me. Birds were singing for me to give me bundles of joy for my wedding. It was wonderful time of the year.

During the ceremony I peeked out to see my husband. (Japanese, wife peeking out to see her husband during the marriage ceremony was not allowed) He was shaking. I could see the sakazuki (a cup had sake which we had to drink for bond) his two hands holding sakazuki, were shaking, and his face was so tight like a rubber band stretched as much as he could. It was ready to snap off.

I was not nervous at all. I was more mischievous than nervous. I had to act gracefully but I didn't. I was not supposed to jump around, but I jumped around. I should walk like a lady, but I didn't. My friends were correcting me for my actions.

They said, "You should act like a lady. You should be more elegant."

I agreed, but I didn't act the way I was supposed to. Maybe I was a little more tomboy to show off to my friends how I was not nervous.

The wedding day my side of family, uncles and aunts, nephews and nieces did not attend. My mother and my sister and her husband (Maki) only attended my wedding. My relatives excuses were, because I Marrying to an American. I had disgraced them. I understood. I did disgrace my family very badly. (We did not believed mix blood especially my family). I was so naïve. I never thought about other people's feeling, and I was so arrogant.

I thought if they were not attended my wedding that was their problem not me, but deep inside of me I had wish I would like to see them in my wedding.

I had many so call my friends, my mother and my sister and her husband they were all attending my wedding that was enough.

I pretended I did not miss my relatives. Wasn't I a librated woman? That I thought I could marry whomever I chose. If they couldn't be happy for my wedding, then good, they did not have to come my wedding. Should I suppose to think that way?

On the wedding night, my brother-in-law

Maki came to my house bringing a case of beer and few bottles of whiskey.

My apartment was very near from my sister's house.

Maki told my husband, "drink," with imitated like he was drinking.

One can of beer to another can. Both were sitting on the floor having a drinking competition. Maki's idea was he tried to get Bob drunk instead Maki got drunk and my husband had to carry him to his house.

This is not the traditional Japanese way. This is Maki's mischievous way. He tried to give me his way to say congratulations. It was good to know Maki's feeling toward Bob.

One day Bob comes home. He was furious, and he told me, "We are not officially married. Do you know that?"

His voice was so loud and very angry. I could feel hot air came out from his breath.

I was surprised by his anger.

Japanese ceremony was not an official

marriage. Even though we both signed our document at the wedding ceremony still needed to be sign again at the town hall. I did not know, and I did not put much weight on about our marriage license. I did not care if I had a license or not.

Bob and I made a trip to town hall, and he made me sign again. That was not important to me. I did not understand why he was so upset about getting a license? Shortly after our wedding Bob moved into my apartment

My place had a one bed room, a living Room and a kitchen, and I had my own bathroom. With Japanese tub (a little square wooden box, but deep tub).

When I sit down in the tub, the water comes to my neck. When I wash my body, I have to get out of the tub; also have a small chair to sit, when I wash my body.

Outside of the tub have good size of the tile floor in the bath room with shower. We wash our self with soap and make clean our body before get in the tub to enjoying warm nice water to relax.

In Japan, many people did not have a place like me. Usually had one room and Share the bathroom (a toilet only). If you pay a little more money, you could have a little kitchen with just cold water sink and a two burner stove no oven no refrigerator.

I was fortunate to had good size of an apartment with four burner stove with good size of refrigerator.

When people wanted to take a bath they usually went to a bath house.

We carry soap with bath towel in the little washbasin and clean clothes.

The bath house, it have the men's bath and the woman's bath there were separated by cashier booth. The bath tub was deep and huge square. Inside of the tub have a narrow step around the tub and then step down to the bottom of the floor. Also you can sit down on the step while you soak your body.

Outside the tub has narrow long seat attach to the tub so when we wash our body we can sit down. Also they have many small chairs to sit while washing your body.

The water was hot and clean.

We clean our body before we going to the tub and we couldn't used any bath towel inside of the tub. You probable pay 10 cents to take a bath, at that time I think. I didn't remember actually how much cost, but very cheap to take a bath. When I think back now it was a very fun place and very original.

Our marriage was very good. When we were together I thought we had a great time. I thought our happiness will be forever.

My mother was a big help. She visited me many times. When she visited me she always cooked for me, because I did not know how to cook or how to clean the house.

What a spoiled child was I? My excuse was "my life was too busy." I always eat out, and I never cooked in my whole life, also I had person came my house to help me clean.

I enjoyed my life style. I felt I was a special. I was somebody very important. I could do this extravagant living. I was stood top on the mountain.

I got up early. I made breakfast (toast with real butter and jam also a cup of coffee) and then woke him up. We had breakfast together. We walked to the train station to see him off. And then I walked to the train station to pick Bob up at evening, and we walked home.

We usually stopped at restaurant to have dinner on the way home. After we ate, we walked home, that was our routine.

One day we were at a noodle restaurant. While we were eating, he told me, "This place I could take you every day, every afternoon, because a taste is so good and cheap."(Its cost in American money was probably .50 cents for one bowl of noodles). We laughed.

I noticed people's eyes at the restaurant or on the street everywhere. I felt people's eyes followed me with some disgusting and looking me down. I didn't care. I did whatever I wanted that I thought.

If they wanted to criticism me go head do it. I could live better than them and I could feel freer then they were.

This was a new way of the century, not like the old fashion styles any more. We (woman) can get choose own life style.

I thought I was librated. I was worry free, flying away into the big sky. Nobody could catch me even they tried tied a rope around my neck to keep me down. Nobody could tie me down. I was a free woman. How wonderful life was and I was full enjoying my life.

On the raining day, I brought an extra umbrella to pick Bob up at the train station. I did not want him to get wet. At the train station many wives were doing something like me. They brought extra umbrellas and they were waiting for their husbands to get off from the train.

It was nice atmosphere, even on a raining day. I could feel warmth from their wives. It was wonderful, warm and happy to see these people, even their temporarily happiness.

When she gets home, she would have to face her mother-in-law. It was very tough. But these couples enjoyed this moment of happiness and they enjoy to the fullest. (In Japan usually wives live with husband and his mother in the same house, and wife should obey to his mother and work hard as much as she can). I was so fortunate. I did not have to live with my mother-in-law. What a relief!

One evening Bob told me," I went to a restaurant with Maki, and we stood of the restaurant watching the fish tank. outside Maki asked me, "Which fish do you like. So I picked the biggest fish, than we went inside the restaurant. Here comes a plate with a whole a fish from head to tail with some garnish. It was the fish I picked.

The fish meat cut into small pieces and put back on to the fish (this fish had a main bone connecting head to the tail.

The chef had removed fish meat very carefully. There was no damage to the inside of the fish. The fish meat was put together to reconstruct the whole fish. The fish looked like it had never been touched. That show how super talented the chef was.

When we started eating it tasted really good until the fish's mouth started to opened and closed, and the fish's tail went up and down. When I saw the fish moved I couldn't eat at all." he laughed.

I was surprised "you lived this country long enough, and nobody took you to a fish restaurant?" But I did not tell him. I just smiled at him.

One evening bob took my mother, my sister and I to same fish store he went before, and he order exactly same the big fish, here come whole fish head to tail prepare same as he had a fish before it put front of us.

I looked my mother and my sister's face. There face tell me how uncomfortable of this dish. Now I know they were not enjoy this fish same as me.

When bob saw our an awkward face he laugh so hard just like this was a big joke to him.

He told me almost every day how happy he was. "I loved Japan and Japanese people."

He said. "Japanese are so kind and nice people also hard worker and well discipline. This country is a super clean country. I do not want to go back to America to live," and I believed him.

One day Bob received a telephone call from America. He said to me, "Black people from my neighborhood are acting very badly, and my mother needs me to come home."

Then he told me, "I have to go home."

I did not understand about black people or American people. I did not understand why his mother wanted Bob to come home for such a minor problem? Couldn't she take care of her house or miner problem ? She was a grown woman. She should took care like this little problems instead asking her son to come home. Bob was working. Didn't she want him to be worry free? Couldn't she let him work his job instead of rushing home? That was I thought. I felt a little strange about his mother because in Japan even with a life threatening problem parents never asked favors to their children.

We just let our children be worry free. We took care of any business ourselves. But I did not tell him that I had a hard time to understood his mother's request.

I did not worry about him or what decision he made. He was a grown man and he would do what was right. Here in Japan I had my mother and my friends and my business. I was doing extremely well. If he went back to America for a little while or for good that was not a big deal. I know Bob; he will come back to Japan. He enjoyed in Japan and he won't let Japan to go away.

When I saw Bob's worry face, I told him, "Why don't you go home and see what is going on in the America."

He thought for a few days then he said to me, "I have good idea, why don't we go to honeymoon in the U.S.A. for a month and see my mother?"

I thought this was a nice idea but I had so many reasons why I was not able to go to America. We discussed this quite a few times back and forth. But Bob won.

We had to go to the American embassy in Kobe to get my passport.

When we were in the Embassy, a lady with a concerned face asked me, "Is he a widower?" She spoke to me in Japanese.

"Maybe he has a wife in the U.S.A? When you get to America maybe you will be not be able to come home. Are you sure you want to go U.S.A. with him?" She was very concerned.

When I think back now, we had big problems with American solder and Japanese women. Maybe that was why she was concerned about a Japanese woman who had married an American.

Many Japanese women got a passports and marriage licenses, and she spend all her life saving on her husband, but when the day came for the husband back to America, he usually left in Japan without wife and his children and never return to her.

The woman in Japan believed her husband's promise and waited with her baby about her husband to come back to her. But husband never come back.

Many Japanese women were suicide because of shame and lost hope. Also many

Americans soldier already had a wife in the USA. I though these situations were not me, never happen to me. I thought many Japanese women were so stupid.

She said to me, “This marriage license does not tell me anything. Does he have a wife or not?” she told me with a worried face.

Bob was very upset and told her his first wife was dead. I knew this and I knew he had three children. His mother was taking care of them.

After leaving the embassy we walked around Kobe. This town we called an exotic town. Many foreigners lived here.

The houses were built in the American style with a lot of windows and big kitchens. They had living rooms with many couches. The bathrooms had Japanese tubs with showers. The bedrooms had bedroom sets with side tables and lamps. There were more like American up-level house. They were big house and usually had second storey. The house had big yard with lawn.

On the streets, many foreigners were passing buy. Some were black people, Some were European, and some were Chinese and Korean, Pakistan, Indian and other. There were many different Nationalities and stores were to serving these people's needs.

It was a very unique town. In one part of the town I could hear French music, another part of town I could hear Chinese.

When we were walking though the town, I could hear English. (It was funny to think how all kinds of music blended very nicely).

We had a few days to prepare to leave Japan.

The president of the Japanese company, where Bob worked, begged Bob to come back and work for them.

"I will come back to Japan." bob said to the president.

He and his company's coworkers told me,

"How lucky I am." Another person told me "You can come home to Japan to live and visit the U.S.A. every year for your vacation. It's awesome."

Before I left Japan, I gave my store to one of my stitches. She was my best worker, and I knew she would keep my customers happy.

This was a Japanese custom for those who had worked hard and had done a good job, and had worked for their boss about twenty years or more. The business owner usually made a new store for these persons and help them the business to grow.

On the day we were going to leave Japan many people came to say goodbye to us at the airport.

I saw my mother's face. It was very lonesome. She tried to smile at me, but her mouth was shaking and I saw tears in her eyes.

At that time I did not pay much attention because I was so excited about my trip. I never thought that this was my last trip, or that I might not be able to come back to Japan in a month. (I think my mother sensed I would not come back to Japan in a month).

I was only thought about I'm going to go to America. I thought I will have a wonderful time. I was excited. We were going to stop in Hawaii on the way to America. It was awesome.

IN FLORIDA

My husband and I arrived to the airport at Miami Florida almost 40 years ago.

I was 26 years old gullible and *hakoiri musume (*grow up with silver spoon) with a lot of ambitious than. Now I think back myself I realized how defenseless and did not know how the world existence. I was live own world. I thought I was an extremely intelligent and hard worker so I could handle any situation well and I will capable to do whatever necessary that I thought myself. How naïve I was.

I thought my dress was very sophisticate.

I wore a white silk tank top with short sleeve and a black skirt with black enamel high heels, and I wore a black big brim hat. I carried small rectangular handbag the same color as the shoes to mach. Also I wore white short gloves, and I had a Japanese fan to give me some air and cool me down on that hot day.

When I was in Japan I lived and acted like celebrity. I had enough self confidence about my job more than any other people. I was a stuck up very much and an obnoxious very young woman. I did not realize about other people's feeling or how important to understood other human been. I thought I was the best for everything. Even though I had enough confidence myself, I was a little nervous to be visiting Bob's mother.

I knew it was our honeymoon and just one month visit. That was our agreement before we left Japan. That was why I had agreed to visit the U.S.A.

When I arrived in America, I found out my English was not good. I realized that, even though, I had gone through an English intensive course in Japan before I came to this country, but I realized I learned much different English here than the English I had learned in Japan. I understood a little English language, but I was not able to speak at all. I was useless that made me terrified.

Before we left Japan, Bob told me, "After we visit my mother we are going back to Japan to stay. We are going to live near your family." He loved Japan.

Before we left Japan my mother told me, "I am going to build a house as wedding present for you and your husband to live in, while you're visiting U.S.A. as a honeymoon."

My mother's news was a big and wonderful surprise! I was very curious about what kind house my mother would build. Would be Japanese style or American? Maybe half would be Japanese and half would be American style? I looked forward to seeing my future house. That made our trip to the U.S.A. more enjoyable, and I would something look forward to come home to.

I loved to see many different countries. I loved to explore in my young life as much as I could. I always had curiosity of everything. Like curiosity cat. I was excited. I had gone to Thailand, Hong Kong and Singapore, but I never visited America. I thought, "This trip would be a marvelous trip for us. I was delighted."

On the way to America, we stop in Hawaii. Beautiful crystal clear water and we sat on the beach look sun going down. The Weather was lovely and sunny with dry wind.

Bob rented a car looked like a toy car. It looked like a jeep but did not have a roof or door. It was fun to drive around in Hawaii. Our hotel had Welcome party for Japanese tourists. Bunch Japanese were gathers stood around pig barbeque.

Hotel employees prepare whole pig. They bury pig 8 hours in the sand and let sun to cook then they took out pig tied to a pole. They brought pig over the fire and cook for another few hours. I had never seen pig barbeque before it made me very interesting.

We went to international market to see different items and much different kind of people. We went to the bird zoo to walk thought in the cage. There were so many wild birds fly over us. I was scare of that.

We walked around the beach to see hula dance. We had a wonderful time and awesome memory to start our honeymoon.

First time Bob introduce me McDonald. This was the American food. I thought a cup of milk shakes was awesome. We (in Japan) did not have milk shake and very few people drink milk. My mother used to tell me how awful smell milk was.

We stayed in Hawaii three days and then

we left to America.

We arrived at Florida airport. It was a very hot and muggy. It was very strong sun scorched over the airport at that day. At the airport Sunny Bob's older brother was waiting for us.

The first time I saw Sunny, my thought about him was "what a nice good looking man. "Also what kind of physical work out does he do? His body was well-built and very attracted a man. He was awesome!"

When Sonny saw us he approached to my husband and started talked to him. But he never said any words to me as matter of fact he just ignored me. *I thought that was not polit. In Japan we never ignored people.*

He talked continually from the airport all the way to Bob's house in Hometown Florida. Actually he never shut up.

I was amazed how men could talk like him. I knew women could talk a long time but some men could talk even more than women! Japanese men speak a very briefly do not talk a long time like him.

When we arrive to my husband's house I found out my husband had a beautiful house with big swimming pool in an extraordinary neighborhood. His house had many colorful flowers and many green bushes in his back yard and around the swimming pool. It was beautiful.

Front of his house had a lot of different kind of tropical flowers and trees too and add tasteful landscape made just breathtaking. Bob's house was very small compared to the neighbors. They were tasteful, nice big houses and they were like mansions to me.

His house was surrounded by judges, doctors and lawyers. I was impressed.

The house was paid in full. Bob's house originally had three bedrooms, two bathrooms, a living room, a garage and a kitchen with a breakfast table. There was a window cut in the kitchen open to the pool side. This made a counter for people to sit and have something to drink or to eat and enjoying poolside.

The Back yard was very big and it had a fence around a big swimming pool. There was a screen wall and roof surrounded the swimming pool. So no bugs could come into the pool. Many flowers and many trees were tastefully planted around the swimming pool made more attractive. In Front of the house had very big yard Where a big boat was parked. Flowers were everywhere. It was gorgeous. The bright Florida sun helped grow flowers. There were a cheerful and pleasant atmosphere and nice breeze made me welcome. It made me comfortable, and I felt a wonderful welcome.

The living room was a quite a large room open to the kitchen. The other side had a sliding door open to the swimming pool. The opposite side of the sliding door opened to a living room to hallway.

The living room had a couch and love seat and There were side tables in between the couch and love seat and on each side of the couch and love seat. Each these tables held lamp also There were two lazy- boy chairs side- by- side facing to big TV. Between the lazy boys was a table and lamp. There were two floor lamps one on each side of the lazy-boy chair.

The garage was converted to be our bedroom.

Bob's mother occupied the master bedroom. It had a big bathroom and a walk in closet. It was really big closet. You could have made another room this closet. Bob owned this house. His mother lived here free. She was supposed to be taking care of Bob's three children.

These children had more than million dollars trust. Because their mother dies few days after she discharge from the hospital. They settled huge money to her children in trust.

Now Bob mother is in charge of this trust and Bob's paycheck too. She received his paycheck directly from his company. Also Bob paid all the house expenses.

Bob had three children. Jack was four, Nancy was seven, and Tom was ten years old.

Bob's sister Betty and her baby Lisa, two years old and her new baby and my husband and I. Also his mother and her husband were lived under one roof.

I become the instant mother of these three children as well as maid and live-in baby sitter. I did not know at the time that I was going to do all this work. I was also a few months pregnant. I was determined to have the baby in Japan.

It would be so nice to have my baby in Japan. My mother could help me and teach me how to raise my baby in the old fashioned Japanese way. I think old- fashioned

Japanese way, was a better way. I always believed. I believed Bob's promised that we were going home to Japan after we visited his mother. I was looking forward to going back to my home Japan. I was believed in him that he would take me back home to Japan soon.

The first two weeks in Florida were wonderful like I was in dream.

Bob took time off from the company. He was home with me to enjoy our married life. It was awesome. Every morning I got up with big surprised. He made me a breakfast in bed, I never had custom to eat food in bed and I was not adjusted well at all.

I heard Bob's mother said to Bob, "You shouldn't bring breakfast to her let her come to the kitchen."

Some other time he made a Japanese food miso soup for me special. I was surprised how he knows how to make Japanese food, and I felt I was most important woman for his life.

While Bob was home, we went to many places' every day. To Miami and drove around downtown. Also he drove around the countryside of Hometown to shopping mall, and we went to a movie. Much more we did fun things.

Also we visited one of Bob's friends, whom came from Cuba. Bob started talking Spanish to him a little bit. We spend whole day with him and his family. We had wonderful time.

Another day we took the three kids and put blankets in the car went to a drive-in movie. A drive-in move was a first time experience for me. In Japan we did not have drive-in movies. It was mysterious to me, how could you sleep while watching movie? The movie support to be enjoyed not sleeping.

Today was very hot day. We were at the swimming pool enjoying cold water to cool us down. I did not know how to swim

Bob put a float around my body and let me practice to float. While I was practicing Bob disappear a little bit then I saw him farther side of swimming pool and he hold up my float. As soon as I saw it I sunk under water. He told me, I was floated a little while and if I practice I will able to swim soon.

At evening we went a night club to dance.

I hated going to an American restaurant or night club. Japanese night clubs and the American night clubs were much different.To me American night clubs were dirty and dark. It was too dark couldn't see any seem like hiding something and the smoke filled the room and it made a sheet of fog that made me choke and smelled horrible. Also there was no good food to eat.

They did not have an orchestra to play nice music and did not have a beautiful floor to dance. The seats were very uncomfortable and not fancy at all.

Many American people were drunk and acting silly and wasted. Also their dresses were disgusting and they did not behave well. The band was a horrible sound. It was much disappointed and not for night out to enjoy.

Japanese night club, all seats were stuffed clothes or leather seats. It was beautiful and comfortable seats to sit like living room furniture. When we went to a night club, we wore nice fancy clothes, and we were very quiet. We watch people beautiful dancing like ballroom dance. We listen to wonderful music. We really enjoy being there.

The club's foods were always very delicious. Any night clubs are places to enjoy and they cater to the customers. Also men go to the night club, but not for woman, but sometime husband or friend bring woman to the night club.

In the night club there were many beautiful women work there to entertain for men.

Another night Bob took me to a Chinese restaurant. The outside and inside of the restaurant looked very fancy. It seemed like a very expensive. A waitress had just finished cleaning the table and we sat. I putted my hand on the table. It was sticky and dirty. “yak” it was disgusting and still wet, before complete dry a table. The waitress had thrown silver ware on to the table instead of putted them on the table neatly.

I was surprised! I hesitated to sit down and had dinner there. I saw the water glass had some kind of stain liked it was foggy. The silver ware had water stained too. The food tasted horrible and disgusting. It was a very big disappointment.

The waitress or waiters were not polite to customers at all. They argued with the customers any chance they got. They made many mistakes with our food.

I pointed out her mistakes to the waitress. The waitress said to me, “so, I am human!" that answer shocked me.

We never ever say such rude words to customers. We apologized even, if the customers were wrong.

In Japan we never left any table wet. We washed the table completely cleaned and dried them. Any Japanese restaurants were super cleaned. Tables were spick-and–span. You could eat off from the tables. Also there were no bad smells. Even in cheap Japanese restaurants the food was excellent taste and the places were clean. They put chopsticks very neatly. It looked like they measured before putting on the table.

When we sat down on the chair in the restaurant, the waitress brought warm neatly folded hand towel(like face clothe size)to the custom, so they could clean their hands before relaxing.

Even in the cheaper restaurant they had to bring a clean, warm, towel. Warm towel is for winter and cold towel for summer.

Japanese restaurant employees were very nice, polite, sincere and honest. They tried to help customers and take time as much as they could. They made sure to keep the place cleaned without being told by their employer.

They always looked for something to do to help their employer.

Waitress or waiter never made mistakes with the customer's order or argued back with the customer. They were always humble.

Outside of the restaurant have a display case made from wax exactly same as real foods were displayed to show sample of menu to customer. So even you do not speak the language you get exactly what you want you can get it.

In Japan we do not tip the waitress or waiter. It was quite different between Japan and the U.S.A. It was the beginning of my experiences in the U.S.A.

WHILE I LIVE WITH LINDA

Our wonderful honeymoon was over. We had a super wonderful and happy time. It went by too quickly.

Today is my husband first day back to company. He won't be home for two weeks. Even thought he left the house for work two weeks, I felt his kind and warm. I still feel about his sweet and tenderness. I knew he tried to spoil me.

We had good time together and I have to hold on his sweet and warm feeling until he will be back home, and I couldn't wait. But I have to wait.

As soon as my husband left, Linda told me my duty was to taking care of his children.

I don't mine but I really needed little time to adjust my situation. But Linda's word was very important to me, and I would like to work harder for her. I wanted to her to like me. I will do whatever she said.

I got up early enough to wake children up. When I started making breakfast, Linda came to the kitchen and sat in the chair she just watched me.

I didn't know what I was doing, because I never cooked food before in my whole life. I was very nervous especial Linda was watched me, But I tried harder to please her. I thought she maybe show me how to make American breakfast.

I put cereal in the bowl and pour milk then I gave to children. Nancy asked me "kazuko did you put sugar in cereal?" I said "Am I supposed?" Nancy said, "you should." so I gave sugar bowl to them to put sugar themselves.

While they were having breakfasters I made three ham and cheese sandwiches and some fruits and bottle of milk put in their lunch boxes ready to take to school.

As soon as Linda saw me she yelled at me. "Stop" loud as she could. I stopped right away and wait what Linda had to say.

She told me, "Kids did not need ham & cheese sandwich. They should have peanut butter and jelly is good enough."

I did not know what peanut butter was. Her complain actually surprise me.

Nancy showed me very disappointed face. Somehow I made over sandwiches.

It still had time to school bus to come, so we went to the living room. Linda already sat at the chair and watching TV. So we tried to watch TV. Linda said "This program is not for the kids. You go to kitchen and wait for the school bus to come."

So we move to the kitchen and we sat kitchen chair opposite side of TV so we couldn't see. We waited the school bus to come.

Anyhow I sent kids to school. What a day! I already made first mistake. Oh boy I did not want to do any mistake anymore. I did not understood why I couldn't make good lunch for the kids?

After kids left house. I start making a breakfast for Linda. I tried to put cereal in the bowl before I pour milk. I got big shouting voice again. "What are you thinking? I am not kid I need good breakfast. I need bacon and eggs with toast."

I did not know what bacon was. I said myself, "Don't make me confuse please," but I did not tell her. I started cook with wonder how to cook. I hope my cooking would be correct like she requested.

Bacon started brown and crisp like same as I saw Linda was eating before. Hope my cooking was right.

I set a portable table front of the TV and then I brought out the food to Linda. While Linda having a breakfast I cleaned up kitchen. Just I finished cleaning, Betty got up, and she sat at a chair.

I poured coffee and I put a cup of coffee front of her.

Betty told me, "Where is my breakfast? Are you going to make my breakfast aren't you? I want some bacon and eggs with two slice of toast with butter and some jelly. Hurry up cook I am very hungry."

So I started cook again. I had to clean the kitchen again. Finally I finished cleaning then Betty's baby woke up. I brought the baby to Betty. She told me, "Get the formula." I did not know what formula was. I asked her, "What is a formula."She said, "Special milk."I had hard time to figure out what did she mean special milk? I walked around kitchen and open one cabinet to another cabinet looking for special milk. It took me a little while then she said to me, “powder” oh boy what she said powder? “What is powder where can I find powder?”

I saw one can with baby face I open the can I saw powder. I taste it a little bit. I guess maybe this one have to be. Maybe this is what she said to me power milk. Now I guess what formula was what a relief! Then I realized. I didn’t know how to make it. I had to ask her again I felt I was so dumb.

She said “Read information!” Oh my God, I though she knew I couldn’t read English well. Why she said read information to me?

I did not have courage to tell her I couldn’t read English. It was embarrassment, but I had to do my duty. I was in the kitchen and I tried to figure out what to do. I know one bottle but I did not know how many scoop of milk should put into. I was stuck.

Should I put water in the bottle or boiling water? If I put too much water that was not good other hand if I put too much scoop of milk that not good ether.

Oh my God if you were there please helps me to understand this information. Please help me. So I could do my duty without making any mistake please.

I put milk and water then tasted I did over and over to come to just right. Oh yes, I made just right maybe? I hope. I gave it to Betty. I thought she will feed the baby.

She told me, “I am eating. You feed the baby” I never had experience to take care baby. I didn’t know how and I scared if anything happen to the baby. But I must obey her oh well I had to try. What a day? This was new to me and I was very much nervous.

I didn’t realize before I came to this house. I had do change baby’s diaper and clean the house. I was so scared not do mistakes.

I finished cleaning, took me a quite time to finish whatever I have to do. It was almost lunch time.

I started to make lunched for Linda and Betty. They sat at the chair and watch TV while they were eating. I brought their drinks by their request.

Finally I had a little time to sit and grab something to eat. Almost ready to eat one bite of toast, Linda said to me, "you start cook dinner before my husband home."

I did not have a time to eat my breakfast or lunch? then I realized, I was not able to have breakfast or lunch to eat in this house. That ok if I could work without do mistake That was more important for me now.

As soon as I heard Linda's announcement I was nervous. I didn't know how to cook American food. Did I have to cook American way? I did not know my cooking was doing right or wrong. I hope I didn't do any mistake. Anyhow I made their dinner without confidence but seem like they like my dinner. What a relief!

After supper, Youngest grandson Jack asked Linda "Would you read story for me grand mom." with his scare face.

I was not understood why he was so afraid of her. Linda said to jack, "you are too stupid even I read story to you never understand that is waste my time go to bed!" She holds some stick and ready to hit him.

I grab a book, and I went his room. I jumped in his bed and I started read together, because I couldn't read English well, but he and I tried one page a time and we had good time then.

Next morning I start cooking for children. I saw beacon and egg in the refrigerator so I started cook for them.

Linda came to kitchen she scolded me again. "Don't you know kids do not need to eat bacon and egg? It is too greasy and not good for them they just have cereal is enough." When I made breakfast for kids, but I was not allowed to sit down with them to have the breakfast.

She said to me, "you have so many thing to do you don't have time to sit down and Have the breakfast." Oh well my stomach growling louder and louder.

I was pregnant. But Linda would not allow me to have food, unless my husband was home. I was always hungry. After few months pass, I realize I was not able to wear sundress anymore, because my bone was sticking out and showed sick looked, my face was so skinny, my eyes were pup out like a monster. It was too big on my face and scared people. Even see myself in the mirror I was shock. How could let myself became this sick looking.

In the middle of the night no one here, everybody went to bed little earlier than normal time. No sound around I could heard wind blow and rain tapping the window to talked to me. I realized I was hungry. When I thought the food my heart started racing. maybe I could eat something. “Goodly.” I sneaked in the kitchen, and I opened the refrigerator. I was so nervous, because I sat in the kitchen chair with one slice of American cheese. My body started trembling. I removed plastic cover very carefully not make any sound. I felt I was doing something wrong, and I felt I was stealing something. I felt very guilty. But I ate a slice of cheese little bit a time tried to made last longer as much I could. I enjoyed it, and I ate slowly my feast. It tasted super good. It was super delicious and melted into my mouth. I felt like I was flying to heaven, and luxuriated it. I felt this was the food. But I was so Scar my heart was pumping.

I hoped no one would wake up to catch me while I was eating my feast. Hope no one heard sound of chewing my food.

It sacred but it was wonderful taste. It gave my stomach little bit of satisfaction and felt good.

I did not like to eat cheese, when I was in Japan. I hated it. I never developed taste of cheese before. But now I ate this feast and I was so happy. I went to bed with happy. I was so relief to eliminate of hungry and gave a little bit of satisfaction in my stomach.

That day was a very happy day for me.

Next early in the morning I heard somebody screaming. Linda spoke loud as could be.

I went to the kitchen. I did not know what she was saying. I never thought she was talking about me. Come to realized, she was talking about one slice of American cheese I took last night. That she was talking about.

I did not know a slice of American cheeses made such a big problem. She let everybody to know especially me what happen while there were sleeping.

"Who ate my chesses? Do we have a thief in this house?" She looked at me with hate in her eyes and she pointed at me with her finger. Because of me missing a cheese.

This incident happened at Bob's house before we moved into this trailer and I was pregnant.

MY MOTHER IN LAW

I know Japan, when woman get married, she treated husband's mother and family better then own mother. Do not complain. Do not ask any question tried work harder. That way we were.

I tried taking care of his children extremely good and worked hard as much I could, but between us (Linda and I) we didn't understand each other. When I worked harder I dug ditch deeper and deeper between us every single day.

Maybe I did not understand her way or

American way. I did not appreciated Linda talk about me how I was useless or I did not know American way to my neighbors.

When my husband home, Linda made a dinner and I could sit at dining table with them. Only then I could have second plates.

Usually I was not allowed to sit dining table. Linda talked to me so sweet when Bob was home. She asked me, "Kazuko would you like to have another plate?"

I was tried to say no, but my hungry was won. I was usually not allowed to eat any extra food because it was cost too expensive. That she would say.

Remember I was pregnant. I needed a food. I needed a lot of food and milk to feed my baby growing inside of me and make sure my baby have strong bone. Also, I needed a peace in my heart to give my baby nourishment for mental emotional support to grow health and strong and smart baby. None of these requirement I did not have and I always starving. It was nature to me I grab food whatever I had chance for second plate.

Linda told Bob, "kazuko eat like garbage disposal. She eats a lot. I didn't know where she puts on all food she eats. She seems like never enough to full her stomach. Maybe she has a hole in her stomach." Linda was smiling. I never saw her smile face before.

Everybody laugh, I saw Bob's face, he looked happy, I think, he thought I was taken good care of. Didn't you know I was losing weight every day? Didn't you know I was getting sick looking?

One day my husband brought home two big size box of Japanese food for me, and he went back to work for two weeks. As soon as he left for work, Linda invited so call friends. She asked me, front of her friend, "Kazuko you have too many Japanese foods why don't you make something for us, so we could taste your nice Japanese food."

I fall again with her request. Before I started cooking I brought out Japanese cracker and some pastry with Japanese tea and then I started cook food for therm.

I was in the kitchen and bring out one dish to another. Each time I brought food Linda said, "Kazuko do you have another way to cook Japanese food and you should bring many different way of Japanese food so we enjoy your food."

I cooked different many meals and another dish to until I used up all my groceries.

This was her request. I never had any chance to sit down to eat with them. Also Japanese custom woman cook dinner but she was not allow to sit with guest and have dinner together. Woman stay in the kitchen guest sits in the dining table with house owner usually husband, but this situation house owner would be Linda. Linda knew our custom. She heard from Bob.

By the time I finish my cooking, and I came to dining table, and I tried to sit and relax a little bit. Linda told me, "Kazuko my friend would like to take whatever left over, would you put these all food put in some container and give it to them."

I was disappointed. But I did whatever Linda's requested. I had put all food in containers and I brought out many containers for her friends.

It was torture for me to my favor Japanese food pass by me. After I packed and gave away. I realize all my grocery were gone which my husband brought for me special, then I realized how stupid I was (maybe to be honorable)?

I cooked food for them, but I had any chance to taste any of my Japanese food. This was only I could had a chance to enjoy Japanese food and I Missed it.

When Bob was not home, I was not allowed to eat any food except Linda gave me some leftover for me to eat. I was not allowed to have second plate or any snack.

I was a pregnant. I was always hungry. I did not gain any weight whatever I ate, that keeps my baby alive but not enough food to be grown strong and healthy baby. I think my baby was survived because my friend Keiko.

One evening at dinner table, my husband asked his mother, “Would you take kazuko to buy a diamond ring? I never had a chance to get her our engagement ring for her. If you take her shopping I will love you more” and then he left next day for work.

Linda took me to a mall. Actually she was enjoyed her shopping instead take me to the jeweler store. We walked half way in the mall. This mall was very big mall I thought I never get jewelry store. They had many nice jewelry stores but look expensive. She decided to go this cheap jewelry store.

In the store Linda told me, “This is a good ring don’t you think so.”

It looked awful. Stone had crack and color was not bright at all. It was terrible.

I hesitated to answer her.

She told me, “Why don’t you answer me? You don’t like because I decide what kind ring you are allowed to have? You should appreciate with me, because I took my valuable time to take you shopping.”

I did not know how to answer her nice way so I just shut my mouth and kept quiet.

But the time to pay the money Linda told me, “Kazuko you still have some money left from your mother aren’t you? You should pay this ring and I will tell your husband when he will get home, and I will get money for you. So I did pay the money for my ring. Also I did not like to argue with her.

When my husband came home and at dinner table Linda said, “Kazuko show your nice ring I got for you.”

I wave my hand to my husband. He was smiling.

Linda said to Bob" oh boy your wife was a very difficult woman to take her shopping. We walked in the mall one end to another. We walked all day to find this ring and which was very expensive ring she had a very expensive taste."

He gave her money what she told my husband but I never see Penny from her.

I did believing Linda. She couldn't be mean to woman, who has a child by her son? My baby would be her grandchild. I believed she would be a reasonable person. She would support my pregnancy. I trusted her. I did not argue with her anything comes between us. She was a Bob's mother how thing will go wrong. She will take care of me good. No reason to be question about her that I thought.

I get up very early morning every day, before sun come up. I prepared breakfast for family. I made breakfast for the kid. I was getting used to have a toast or few peace of cereal here and there to pup into my mouth. I swallow cereal without milk or piece of toast without butter before Linda came to the kitchen. I tried very quiet and I had to eat very fast. I was supplied my action.

I never sneaked around my food I came before this house. I never eat poorly. I had a pride and I did not know what hungry was. I never felt afraid to eat food before.

Now looked at me I was not myself anymore. I lost my manner. I was so nervous, when one spoonful of food put in my mouth I had to look around made sure nobody there to look at me.

I felt like a thief breaking into somebody's house. Maybe not same, but I felt so guilt. I was shaking. Hope Linda won't found me I was eating food.

I went to the children's room to wake them up made sure they washed their faces. I helped them to found clothe to wear. It was so hard to found clothe for them because they did not have good clothes at all. Their clothes were very trash looked and wrinkle all over and looked like never washed them and smell horrible. (This was before I started to buy their clothes).

While children eating breakfast I made three lunches for them to take to school. When time to leave, I told them hurry, hurry," I had to drag them out from the house. I stand outside of the house to see kids getting in the school bus and went to school safe. Kids told me, "Before nobody waited school bus with us." That news was made me shock.

After kids went to school, my first job was done then I started cleaning the house and then I started cook for Linda. While Linda having her breakfast, I started to wash clothes for the whole family. Then I had to take care of Betty's baby.

I washed Lisa (Betty's baby girl two year old) and Betty's baby. I fed them. I put her in the playpen and then I started cleaning the house again. When Linda finished her breakfast I started cleaning the kitchen again. Seem like get dirty so quickly.

I was not allowed to using egg and bacon for children's breakfast. When I cooked for Linda or Betty I had to use eggs and bacon.

At lunch, I started to made sandwiches for Betty and Linda. While I was making their sandwich Linda came in the kitchen to watch me.

I thought she was going to teach me how to make lunch for their way. But I realized why she came to the kitchen for. She made sure I didn't take any pieces of ham or cheese for myself to eat.

I was allowed to eat one slice of peanut butter and jelly. I never had peanut butter and jelly in Japan. I develop the taste and I started to like them that made Linda upset. After they finish their food, I clean dishes and kitchen then I was able to go for walk for short time.

Another morning Nancy brought hair brush and she asked me weather I would comb her hair or not. I say, "I am glad" I started to comb Nancy's hair. Linda told me she will comb her hair because of her hair was so tangle it hard for me to comb so I gave her the hair brush. I went to the kitten to clean up, as soon as I reached the kitchen I heard a scream. I rushed out to see what was going on; It was Linda try to comb Nancy's hair. I saw the hair brush with a bunch of Nancy's hair.

I saw Nancy's face and it made me scared. She did not cry, not even one drop of tear ran down on her face, but I could tell Nancy was so angry and hate. I didn't know what to do but I felt so pained and sorry for her.

Betty

My husband's youngest sister Betty, had blond hair and a flat face with a square chin, and she wore big glasses. Many times I saw her wash her hair in the kitchen sink before she went out, but I never saw her take a shower as long as I remember. (*I think she was not an ordinary person.)* When she opened her mouth, she never shut up whether people were listening or not. She spoke to me, it was very slowly. She did not speak correct English at all. She talked to me like I was retarded. She just picked vocabulary like, "You cook, I eat."

She spoke like a person who did not have any teeth. Just air came though her mouth and sounds disappeared somewhere inside of her mouth. Her sounds slipped away before I could catch what she said.

She was a pretty girl. But her obese body did not help her looks. Heavy drinking and heavy smoking did not help her either.

She always had many different male friends. She was a very bad housekeeper and lazy, but she was a party girl.

One day I had a very innocent question, and I did asked her, "Don't you mix up your friend's names because you have so many different guests come and go at your house? It's like a bus station."

She loved to go to a bar and get drunk any chance that she had.

One day she surprised me got up early for her. It was late morning. Since I had lived in this house with Linda and Betty, I had never seen her up this early. One later morning, she decided to go for a ride, so she told me "Kazuko, go car." She pointed to herself and made motions driving a car. So I knew what her meaning.

I loved to go and see different places. I was excited. I say to myself "she will take me with her to go for a ride!" I was extremely happy! I couldn't explain my feelings. I was more than excited. I was not able to think about any other reason than go for a ride to an unseen place. I went out of the house with enthusiastic. I was very naïve. I did not know why she will take me for ride with her?

I didn't care what she thinking. I just get out this house for a little while.

We drove to the countryside of Hometown. It was a wide open empty road, a very big and a very long road, that seemed like it would never end. The Florida sun shined vividly on my face. The wind came through the window and played with my hair, making it dance around in the air.

I tasted the sweet wind and smelled the refreshing country air. It was just wonderful! The combination of wind and sun were just perfect and awesome.

The wind picked up dirt from the road, it flying around and chasing our car, throwing dirt at me and telling me, "Hey, wake up!"

How naive I was! I still did not realize what was going to happen.

After we drove though long desolate road, we came to a cabbage farm. It was huge. Cabbages made lines very neatly like a military parade. I couldn't see end of this farm. The sun was nourishing all the cabbages and making them very happy and growing healthy.

Betty told me near the field, "We go." We parked our car on the road beside the cabbage farm She told me, "Picking is ok in the US." She told me "Picking cabbage as many as you want. There are too many cabbages in U.S.A." This seemed to make sense to me. It was kind of understood (I felt funny, but I did believe her). I thought, what a different system this country then we were Japan.

Then she told me, “Stand up, if you see a car or people. You tell.” Before I say a word she disappeared somewhere in the farm. I didn’t know why I stood up the road and watched for cars, or somebody coming. Had she told me the truth? Were we allowed to pick cabbage? Why did I have to watch? Why?

It was puzzling to me but I did obey her order. There was a big road running between the fields. Miles and miles seemed to go on forever. There were no houses at all. I saw nothing Just a big desolate place.

There was a big tree here and there. These made shadows and added some color and life to this empty place. It was very quiet and peaceful. The sun scorched the earth. Steam came up and danced wild. The sky was a crystal-clear blue. The sun was so strong I felt I was in a hot sauna. Sweat came out all over my body. I felt like my skin was burning too. A nice breeze sweeping me away for a little while, I did not have a hat to wear.

In Japan I used to wear a hat or use a sun umbrella. Now I wore a sundress. Being few months pregnant kept me hotter and uncomfortable. This was not helping me to keep me cool. But this peaceful isolated place gave me a peace. I forgot to be unhappy.

was enjoying the peace and quiet very much. let myself bathe in the Florida sun. I listened to the birds singing and lost myself in the tranquility for quite a while.

I didn't know how much time passed. All of sudden I saw a car coming our way. The car was very small like a miniature toy car. The sun glittered around the car. The dust was flying around the car trying to cover it over and hiding the car in the dust. It was still quite a long way

I told Betty, "Betty a car is coming." As soon as she heard my voice, she rushed out of the field and jumped in the car then we left.

I did not understand what was going on Just now. Why had she rushed out and taken off in such a hurry?

When we got home, Linda saw the cabbages. She and Betty started talking and Linda decided to make cabbage soup. This was a strange. I couldn't believe she actually would cook!

Same night my husband found out about our trip to the cabbage field. He was very upset and told Betty, "No more taking my wife with you."

After little while I found out that I was not an American citizen at that time. Therefore the U.S. government could ship me out from America and send back to Japan. That's what I heard.

Few days passed. I knew Betty loved Mexican food and she liked to go to a Mexican restaurant.

One night she asked Bob again, “Can I take Kazuko to a Mexican restaurant?”

He gave some money and his car key to Betty. He told Betty. “Do not get my wife in any trouble while you are taking her to the Mexican restaurant.”

His face was very serious and concerned. But we left.

When we got to the place, it was a small dirty Mexican restaurant. In the place was a lot of smoke. It made layer of screen and smelled horrible. It was a cheap atmosphere. We ate some kind of Mexican food. It was hot but surprise it was very tasty.

Next day, Betty asked my husband again. “Is it all right to take kazuko to the bar?

He gave her money and the car keys again and told her, “Enjoy but don’t get in any trouble. Especially don’t get my wife in trouble."

She agreed and we left the house.

On the way to the bar, she told me, "When we get to the bar, a few men will be standing outside of the door. If they ask you any question. You just say you don't understand in Japanese. OK?"

I nodded my head. I did not know why I had to speak Japanese to him or why I had to pretend I did not understand English, but I agreed to do what Betty said.

When we got there a few very huge Muscled men stood at the door like Betty said. Their faces made me scared. One started to ask for my ID. He questioned Betty and I. I told the man. "I don't understand." in Japanese like Betty had told me to do. I felt like lost a child. Inside of me I wanted to answer the man in English, and I would like to show my ID. I did not want to make any trouble, but I had promised Betty, so I had to pretend I did not understand English. (Oh boy! the poor man I was truly sorry).

He asked me again I answered with Japanese again repeating this quite few times. I was surprised how patience this man had! Meantime Betty was watching me and laughing. I was very uncomfortable about the way I had to answer to these men.

He had a little patience with my answer but now his patience was gone. He started to show how much my answer irritated him. Finally they were trying to throw me out.

Betty told me with very innocent face, "You should show you're ID this is America. You can't get in without showing your ID."

I felt uncomfortable how Betty treated about me. I showed my green card to a door man. I was very confused. Why was she telling me this? Did she think this was a joke?

We were finally able to go inside the bar. In Japan there was no big man standing near the door when you going to the bar. Also we did not show any ID to prove our age.

In the bar it was dark. There was a lot of smoke and it smelled nasty and it was difficult for me to breathe.

Many men were drunk and that make me very scared. This was not fun at all. I wanted to go home as soon as possible. I did not want to stay in this scary, cheap dirty place. I felt that if I sat down in this chair my clothes would get dirty and germs would get into me. Inside of my head said," Let's go! Let's go home." I wanted to go home.

But reality was that I had to stay with her. We stay quite while. I was so miserable! I watched people in the bar. Some were drunk and they didn't know what was going on. Some people were talking and laughing. Some people were just staring at the glass of beer and smoking.

When we got home I explained to Bob about the doormen and that I was almost kicked out from the bar. Bob was very angry and told Betty, "Don't make any trouble for my wife. I told you that before you went out."

I realized I did not understand American people and American humor.

Bob 'siblings were loved to go to bars and get drunk almost every day which I did not understand at all.

Betty was a lousy house keeper like all of her family, but she had a job. She worked in a hospital as a nurse. I did not know what time she had to go to work or what time she will come home. While she slept or went out I had to take care of her baby. This was my responsibility until Betty woke up or come. home

I asked my husband before my baby born. "Can we go home?" His answered was, you are pregnant and Air Company does not want travel who pregnant near her term."

I did not know Air company' regulation. Another night I told my husband, "I would like to serve this country. I would like to join the military."

He said. "You are not American citizen so our government won't to give you a job." I was a green card holder and permanent resident.

One day Betty was up early afternoon, I asked Betty to watch her baby while I cleaned the bathroom.

Then I asked Betty "Is it all right for me to take bath?" She said, "Why not." Her answer made me so happy and excited. I started humming. I felt great! I was able to take a bath! Awesome! I started scrub bath tub as hard as I could. I was smiling. I couldn't stop smiling.

We Japanese usually take a bath every day like ritually. We take a bath end of the day before go to bed. We sleep clean and refresh body. We do not take a bath when get up in the morning or afternoon. Not before going out. When we take a bath, we washed our body with soap and made our body clean then we get into the tub. When we were in the hot tub, water comes to our neck. We soak our clean body in a small, deep tub. Nice wonderful hot water makes us relax. It was another way to relieve pressure.

Also we take a bath with family together. We used same water. Usually father comes first then mother with kids they were enjoyed all together in the bath room. Also in Japan bath room and toilet were separated.

The bath was very important for Japanese people. Taking bath is a very spiritual. Nourish our spiritual and mind and body. Three minute shower was not for me that Was not enjoyed.

I finished cleaning the bathroom. I run to my room to get my clean clothes. Oh my God! How happy I was. I could take a bath I couldn't stop smiling. I felt like flying and jumping. When I got back to the bathroom the bathroom door was closed. Oh shucks!

I waited for the door to open. I walked in front of the bathroom back and forth holding my clean clothes to my chest as hard as I could. I hoped she would come out of the bathroom soon. She took long, long time. Seem like forever. I thought she never come out from the bathroom.

Finally the bathroom door opened. I rushed into the bathroom with a puzzled mind. Betty usually did not take a shower special a bath?

Anyhow I rushed into the bathroom and I started taking off my clothes, smiling and humming. I was so happy! Finally, I could take a bath in a clean tub. Oh boy I missed bath too long. I needed to take a bath desperately. I had to clean my body, mind, and spiritual. How lucky I was!

Usually I was not allowed to take a bath because it cost too much for the water bill. Also only I was allowed to take shower twice a week not every day. I usually had a three-minute shower. I never thought Betty was taking a bath with her baby.

I happened to notice something in the middle of the tub. Piled up were some brown spots. It was baby's number two!

I was so discouraged. I was so shock and very disappointed.

I had just washed the tub. How could be? I was sad like a little girl just lost something very precious thing.

I asked Betty to help me clean it.

She said, "You want to take a bath, you clean!"I was pregnant and it was very hard to bend and wash the tub.

TOMATO FARM

A Florida summer is hot and humidity. The sun is always glimmering. If you are outside and stay directly under the sun, the sun will scorch you. But if you are under the shade, you will be cool. The sweet wind will swaddle you. A nice breeze makes Florida's weather wonderful and likable, when I compared to the Japan's summer, it is much comfortable here in Florida. The air is much dryer and wonderful breeze sweep me away.

In Japan's summer it is always too much humid and uncomfortable with many, many people. It is makes more uncomfortable, and difficult to spend the summer in Japan.

Today the sun was shining.
The soft, nice breeze wrapped around me to cool me down and made it a little easy to spend a day outside. Birds were flying around me and sang to me with sweet sounds. It was a perfect and wonderful day in Hometown, Florida. It was White clouds spread all over the beautiful blue sky and looked at us with big smiles.

Today my husband was home. It was a special day. It was awesome day. While Bob was home, we went many, many places'.

Other times we pack a few 6 packs beer and cold drink with some sandwiches and we took Bob's three children, his brother Sunny and his sister Betty, we went on a boat ride.

I didn't know until marine patrol catch up to us. I found out, our three children were throw can's coke, sandwiches bag and empty bag of chips to the ocean.

Other night we went dancing with his sibling. This was first time we went out together for dancing and I was excited.

He had been home since Friday afternoon. It was so wonderful to have him home. I made his favor breakfast for him and his children. I sat at the table with them and I was able to have breakfast together for change. What a wonderful time! How nice to have my husband home! When he was not here, my life was miserable.

When I got up Saturday morning, after breakfast, I cleaned up the kitchen. Middle of cleaning, I took a little break. My husband and I sat at the kitchen table. We were having a cup of coffee, spending a few minutes together. It seemed like I was dreaming. This was a special treat for me.

He told me, "We have to do something fun."

I nodded, before he finished his words, I finished up all the morning chores as quickly as possible. Then I sat beside him and waited for what he was going to say.

He told me, “I think we will go for a ride.” As soon as I heard his word I was so happy. His words all of sudden took the dark clouds away from me. These dark clouds started to build up and hang around me ever since I started living with his mother.

I was excited. I was just like a little kid who got a special toy as a big surprise. I felt like I was walking in the clouds. I ran into our bedroom humming with a big smile, and I jumped around in our bed room.

I could not stop thinking what fun we we’re going to have and what clothes I was going to wear. I was sure I wanted to be pretty, not only for myself. I wanted to be pretty for him. I wanted to wear a nice dress to make me look like a lady for him. I wanted to impressive him, I wanted, I wanted, I wanted so much to make him happy and make him proud of me, but it was too hot and I was pregnant. A dress would make me much hotter.

I decided to wear very casual clothes instead of fancy clothes. I wore a tank top with a big red hibiscus flower on white material, and white short pants to go with it. It was simple but comfortable.

I stood in front of the mirror. I said to me, “you look very nice.” I knew my husband will like my outfit. I felt wonderful and pretty.

While I was living in Florida with my mother-in-law, I lost too much weight. I wore a little girl’s size 8 instead of a lady’s size 10.

However she occupied the master bedroom with a full bath connected to it.

We did not have our own nice bedroom. We were living in a garage attached to the house. Bob purchased a good sized mirror and hung it up on the wall for me to use.

I started fixing my hair, and I put suntan

lotion on my face. I looked into the mirror and I saw the face in the mirror was smiling.

I said "hallo" to the smiling face in the mirror. I said, "Today, I feel something very special. It will be a wonderful day, and I will have a super wonderful time." I talked to the face in the mirror with smiling, and I felt liked dancing around the bedroom.

My husband came into our bedroom, and he asked me, "What are you doing? The Kids are waiting for you. Hurry up! We do not have all day." He took my hand, and dragged me out of our bedroom.

I told him, "Today will be a wonderful day! I can go with you, and we can drive around. This is a wonderful!" He just smiled. I asked "Where are we going?" He said, "Well I don't know exactly."

I said, "It doesn't matter where we are going. Just go for a ride and drive around neighborhood with you will be a lot of fun too." I couldn't stop talking. Surprise myself, how could I speak so much. I felt like a kid. I ran into our car. My husband drove a new white mercury sedan. It was a good size for a family car. When we got in the car my husband's three kids were sitting in the back seat, and waiting for us.

Nancy had a freckled face with a big nose and she had a long pony tail. She wore a colorful jump- suite. She always had a book, and she loved to read.

My husband's two boys are very quiet. Tom had brown hair. Jack had red hair like a carrot. They were wearing blue short pants and white dress shirts. They dressed like twins. They looked very sharp.

Today the Florida sun was so hot that steam rose from our car and roasted us.

I sat in the front seat, and I kept humming. I looked out our car's window to see the scenery of Florida. In Florida, there was nothing special to see. The land was flat, and it seemed like it would never end. There were big empty highways, with few stores quite a distance from each other. There were big huge empty place. Few cars passed and went. It was desolate town.

When we were in Florida, it was before the Cuban people come into the USA. The town we lived in was deserted.

The window on my side was open all the way. A cool breeze came into the car. It made my hair dance around and my face was touched gently by the wind. It was wonderful. It was an awesome!

When our car went through the highway, dust and sand flew into the air and landed on my hair, face and all my body. My sticky body caught the sand I felt very dust. My clothes, my face, and my hair felt sticky and heavy and my mouth was full of sand. and my body was yucky! But this was wonderful to me.

I kept looking at the scenery. This big desolated highway was unusual to me. We didn't have anything like this big isolated highway in my native country of Japan. This was something very different from the scenery I was used to growing up.

I was too busy looking around. I wanted to memorize all the scenery. I wanted to make sure I did not miss any small view or forget any detail. I felt like I was taking a video without a camera.

I did not care how hot was. I did not care how empty the place was. I did not care how few people were here.

I looked back to see how the kids were doing. I saw Nancy. She was reading a book in the car. I told her, "You shouldn't read the book in the moving car. It is not good for your eyes." but she ignored me. If she did not want to listen to my advice, I could not push her to stop reading. Maybe she did not understand me what I said to her. Maybe... Maybe, I hope she would listen to me. I just did not want her to hurt her eyes.

In the car my husband was grinning at

me. I looked at him and I thought what a nice looking guy.

Pop music was playing on our radio. It made me comfortable and relaxed me. I knew this song playing on the radio, but I did not know how to translate the title of the song from my Japanese to English. It was very popular in Japan.

I sang inside of my head (I'm not good singer). I moved my body with the music. I pretended I was a big super star. It was nice.

I did not know how long we drove on the highway. All of sudden my husband stopped our car. He asked me, "Do you want to pick some tomatoes? This is a nice tomato farm." H was looking for my permission! It was awesome.

I said to him. "That will be fun. Let's pick the tomatoes." He told the kids. "Everybody get out of the car. We are going to pick few tomatoes."

The kids were so excited they hopped

around, running toward the farm and disappeared.

My husband and I looked at the backs of the kids. They were happy. Just like normal playful kids. We smiled at them. It was a wonderful and happy time just regular ordinary family event. We walked toward the farm.

The farm had about one acre I guess. This was a small farm in Florida.

When we came close to the tomato farm, the three kids were waiting for us.

I saw a short, chubby man, who had a golden sun tan and white hair. He looked warm and friendly. He stood beside the table. The table had a scale and a rusted money box on it. His face was very kind, and he smiled at me.

My husband said to him, "we would like to pick the tomatoes."

The old man asked, "How many bags do you need?"

My husband said, “Maybe a couple of bags.”

The old man gave us a couple of bags and pointed to the middle of the field. He told us which location was best and had the most tomatoes.

My husband told the kids, “listen when you pick the tomatoes bring them to kazuko. She has the paper bags. You can put the tomatoes in the bags so she can collect your tomatoes without squeezing them.”

Before he finished talking, the kids took off. They ran into the field and disappeared.

I started to pick a few tomatoes. They were as red as the color of fire. They were ripe and looked so juicy and heavy. They looked very good and delicious.

I realized I was very hungry. I did not have any food since breakfast, besides I was pregnant too. I needed a lot of food. (You know a pregnant woman always needs a lot of food.) Those tomatoes were so tempting.

I tried to decide whether I should eat the tomatoes or not. It was very hard decision for me and very difficult to not eat them. I tried very hard. I looked at them for a little while. It would not be good manners if I eat tomatoes.

In Japan we never showed other people we were hungry. We did not eat in front of the public. No matter how hungry we were, we always told other people, "Thank you, but we were not hungry, we just finished eating."

I should not eat while we picked tomatoes. That was we consider a good manner. But these tomatoes tortured me! What should I do? Should I eat them? I would be a good mannered like Japanese? Should I forget that I am Japanese.

I fought a long time and I had a long time to think, but temptation finally won. I decided. I will taste just one tomato and I will stop after I eat just one tomato while we were picking.

I started looking around the farm to find some comfortable place to situate myself. When I found the place under the tree I put the paper bag on the ground and then I made myself comfortable. As soon as I sat down I started eating the tomato.

This tomato was so juice and fresh I ate this tomato very fast just like somebody was tried to take my tomato away against my will.

These tomatoes tasted out of this world! They were delicious. They were super delicious after tasted one tomato I was not able to stop eating. I grabbed tomato with both hands Holding firmly and holding tight as I could, and I shoved into my mouth. Tomato seed and juice were dripping on my beautiful white tank top and my white pants. Red stains made some maps on my white clothes My face was red marks around. my lip like a cannibal. I thought maybe I ate this tomato too fast I had to eat slowly. So

I'm able to enjoy. I had to taste this tomato again.

One after another the three children were bringing me their tomatoes. As soon as I received a tomato, I told them with my mouth full tomato, "Go get more tomatoes."

As soon as I told them they ran back to the field. When the kids gave me a few tomatoes, I would hold a tomato and look at it a little bit, and I started to think, "Should I put the tomato in the bag for them or should I taste their tomatoes too." I had hard time to decide. But my hungry won.

I started ate theirs tomatoes one after another. My original thought was, I will taste only one tomato, but the reality was that after I tasted tomatoes I couldn't stop. Temptation was too strong. I was lost my original idea. I lost so called good manner (In Japan, pride come first). I forgot that I was Japanese. I was so hungry not able to think about good manner. Survive first!

I should felt a shamed and embarrassed to be a bad manner like this, but I was so happy that I could eat as much as I could.

I forget about being Japanese. I was able to eat these tomatoes until my stomach was full without any fear. I did not have any time to pick tomatoes anymore I was too busy eating.

The kids come up to me and looked into the bag. Nancy said to me "Kazuko you are eating our tomatoes? We won't have any tomatoes left."Her face was disappointed.

My mouth was full of tomatoes. I tried to say something to her, but I couldn't speak. "I am busy. I do not have time to talk to you. Hurry up get more tomatoes." That was what I thought. I nodded, and pointed to the field and let her know to go and pick more tomatoes.

After she left, Jack and Tom brought me a few tomatoes. They saw my mouth was full of tomatoes, and around my mouth was red just like painted. Tom asked me the same question. "Kazuko are you eating our tomatoes?" I nodded and pointed at the field to let him know he had to go to the field and pick more tomatoes.

He was not happy but he went off to the field. I was enjoying eating fresh, red, juice, ripe tomatoes. This was heaven. I hoped nobody would disturb me. I should make a sign that said, "Leave the tomatoes. Do not disturb."

Unfortunately I did not have a pen or marker. Oh well they would understand me when they saw my face. I was a very busy eating tomato. I did not have any time to talk to them.

I thought "Leave me the tomatoes. Just go and get me more tomatoes. Why don't you understand me? Do not ask me any questions about eating your tomatoes!" That was what I thought but I did not tell them I was in the heaven now. I was too busy eating delicious, ripe, juicy tomato. I was obsession with tomatoes. I was so happy. Leave tomatoes here and go away. Do not disturb me. Please leave me along. Then my husband came to me. The kids must tell him, because he knew I did not have any tomatoes left in the bag.

He said to me "amount of tomatoes you ate maybe our baby will have a red face like a tomato." And he laughed.

I pointed at him too let him know he must Go. "Go pick more tomatoes and leave me alone."

I didn't know how many tomatoes I ate. I ate probably full paper bag of tomatoes maybe more. Finally I was stuffed. I was not able to move anymore.

When my husband saw me, my stomach hurt from eating too many tomatoes. He did not say a word. Just he smiled at me. After I finished eating the tomatoes our bags started getting full, when the bag was finally full. He said to me, "Have you had enough tomatoes? Are you ready to leave here now? Can you walk or should I get a carriage for you?" He laughed. I told him with a serious face, just like nothing had happened, just like I never eaten the tomatoes while we were picking. (You know I was a well mannered Japanese.) "Anytime you are ready, I am ready."

While he went to look for the children I tried to get up but very difficult, and I tried to pick up the paper bag. Instead I sat back down on the ground. I was waited for my husband to come to help me up, but it took a long, long time. I tried again lifting myself up, and I finally I stood up.

Finally the children and my husband come to me. When they came to me, I was already standing and waiting for them.

He said to the children, "we are going."

My husband carried the bags of tomato. He brought them to the old man.

While the old man weighted tomatoes, my husband told him, “My wife is pregnant and was eating tomatoes like obsesses. She must have eaten a whole field, it must be good taste tomato you have in your filed.”

Old man just laughed and pointed at me with very serious face. He told me “Next time you come, I will weigh you first before you go into the field. Then before you leave my field, I will weigh you again then I will charge you!” He made his face little serious, but soon his face changed to a smile.

We all laughed. Old man winked at me. Then he told me, “You have a wonderful day and good luck for your baby. I hope you come back again with your baby.”

My husband carried the paper bags. Everybody walked to our car. It was an awesome day! My stomach was full. I was a happy and satisfied woman.

My husband asked me, “Would you like to drive around a little bit?” I looked at him with an eager face and told him, “Yes we should drive around to see our neighborhoods.”

GO FISHING

I still remember what happened just like it was yesterday.

Bob and I decided to go to fishing just two of us. We talked about and we made plan. He told his mother “we are going fishing.”

Her reply was “kazuko is pregnant. It is not good for her to go on a boat ride especially so far away from home. Just the two of you going fishing is not allowed.” Was she really caring about me or concern?

Bob asked me “what do you think? Is it too much for you to go on a boat ride?”

I insisted, “We should go fishing just two of us. It will be awesome!” My voice was nagging and pleading with him. I did not want to stay in this house while he was home. I did not want him to find out how miserable I was. Also I would like to get out of this house and away from his mother for awhile.

He listened to me, and he tried to make me happy. I felt his warmth. I thought I could spend time with him with nobody else but us. It would be super wonderful.

The next morning we get up at four o'clock. I made some snacks a few can's soda and sandwiches and packed them in the cooler.

I wear blue short pant and blue and red stripe tank top. I pack sun lotion and *flip flops*. We grab the cooler and other necessary and the fishing poles.

Outside was still dark and even in the hot state of Florida the air was cool and comfortable early in the morning.

Were we really going fishing? I couldn't

believe we were actually going fishing just two of us? It was awesome! No one could stop us. We were going! We were going fishing. I was dancing around with humming. I couldn't stop smiled. It would be an amazing day.

His mother was furious when we left the house just two of us.

I could felt her eyes on my back of my shoulder as we went out the house.

The weather was so beautiful sunny day. The sky was beautiful blue and white clouds were swimming around. The waves of Ocean drift away and came back to greeting us and gave me splashes of water for cool me down. It was nice. The sun was very strong and shining on us. Only I heard the waves come and go. It was like I was listening to very quiet, nice music and no other sounds.

It was so smooth and calm. What a peaceful sounds and a Peaceful day. We had a quiet and wonderful time.

I lie down on the deck of the boat to let the hot strong sun shine on me. I bathe in the sun as much I could and the waves hit the boat and give me cool splashes. Let the wind blow over me so soft to make me relax. It was wonderful. The water is so calm and a clear crystal blue and splashes of white. It was beautiful. Not yellow like Japanese ocean. The sun was hot, but a breeze cools us. It was an extraordinary day.

I let Bob catch the fish, while I enjoyed the wind, sun and water. I dreamed that this trip would never end, and I don't want this trip to end. I wanted us to stay in the middle of ocean. We could spend our whole life time here forever. I was dreaming. We were on the boat and he catches the fish. I cook them. We spend whole our life like Robinson family in TV move.

We saw many other boats came and went. We chat a little bit with the other boats that come near us. Some other boats just pass by. It seems everybody enjoys Florida life.

I felt very nice and easy, peaceful and contentment. It was a wonderful day.

We catch many fish, but there were not familiar to me. These fish were bigger and much more different than I used to see in the Japanese fish markets.

That night we brought a lot of fish home. Bob cleaned the fish and we ate. I ate. Oh Boy! I ate such a lot of fish that I couldn't move anymore but it was so delicious. Bob gave some fish to Linda's cat.

It was funny cat that did not like fish. The cat did not come near the fish which Bob put in the cat dish. It was a strange cat like the strange person who owns this strange cat.

keiko

One afternoon my husband asked me, "In your dreams do you speak English or Japanese?" with a grin on his face.

His words made me think. Did I speak English or Japanese? I couldn't figure out what language I was speaking in my dreams. I was losing Japanese but I couldn't speak English either.

He told me, "You can't speak English. Also you are forgetting your own languages. You have to decide which country you are going to be." Of course I would rather speak

Japanese. That was very comfortable for me, and I would rather live in Japan, that I thought.

Recently I was getting irritated over everything I did, because I was not able to communicate with anybody, I felt very secluded. I never had any experience taking care of minor children. I wished my husband would understand how it felt to be my pregnant in a strange country with no one to help me.

I met Keiko few months after I arrived in Florida. The first time I met Keiko was in the store. My first impression was, she was a very beautiful woman and was well dressed, like many Japanese people, and she looked intelligent. She married to an American Army man. She invited me to her house. I was so thrilled to spend some time with a Japanese woman and talk Japanese.

The day I visited Keiko's house, I tried doing my morning chores fast as I could.

I was excited to be visiting her house for the first time. I was nervous and scared. On the other hand I would speak Japanese, and I could express my feelings to someone. I had mixed feelings.

I walked to Keiko's house. When I visited her house it made me surprised. Their shoes were laid on the floor very neatly, and I couldn't see any dust or trash anywhere.

It was very clean like in my country, even though she had two young children. I didn't remember what ages they were, but I would say maybe elementary school age. Her house was Florida style home. One floor no basement or no second floor with chain fence in. In the yard she has a dog running around. Also she has a dog house in her yard and the dog sleep in the dog house.

As soon as I entered her house I felt warm and comfortable and very familiar smell. She was already preparing Japanese tea and Japanese pastry.

We sat at the kitchen table and we started talking Japanese. I spoke like someone who had been isolated from the main land and had never seen people before.

My words come out like a running river so smoothly flowing out very perfectly. Nothing bothered me. I did not have to think before what I said something or wonder what kind vocabulary I should use. What a relief! It was amazing to me.

Each time I visited Keiko's house as soon as Keiko saw me, she started making Japanese tea and started prepare food for me. I enjoyed her Japanese food and few cups of tea. This wonderful treats made me worthwhile to survive and made me I was a human. It was delicious and felt I was in heaven. I thought I would like to visit her regularly if I could. I strongly felt I really wanted to stay here with my friend forever I didn't want go back to that hell house. Even my husband is coming home every other week. His house was not our place to stay anymore.

My friend was very much homesick even her husband was so nice to her and he was a wonderful man and treated her extremely well. When I saw how her husband treated her sweet and kind made me cry. Made me realized how different between me and her same Japanese woman but much different situation.

I was home sick very deeply too. Also, being a few months pregnant made me feel worse than ever. I was extremely lonely and scared. My unknown and insecure future made me even more terrified. What was I suppose to do? I had no one to talk to, and I did not understand English. I did not like being pregnant in this strange country.

At the kitchen table, she said, “One day I was at home watching Japanese TV and eating Japanese food. I happened to look outside of my house. I saw an American man walking down my street. I thought, why is a foreigner walking near my street? What is he doing?' Then I realized this is American not Japan. Of course he is entitled to walk near my house." We laughed.

Each time I visited her, she made me Japanese food. Other days she made snow white, warm, short grain rice and *nori (dry seaweed*.)The rice just came out of a rice cooker; steams were dancing up from the rice. That was my country's food. It looked delicious and it made me feel like I was with my family. She made miso soup with seaweed and tofu. "Oh boy!" it smelled wonderful and She cooked *Saba (*Japanese dry fish) and some special Japanese pickles (*Takuwan* made from *Daikon.*) They were sweet and crunchy.

I had not had this gorgeous real Japanese food for so long. My stomach started growling. And I started drooling.

When she put all kinds of Japanese food

on the table for me to eat, I still lived by Japanese customs. No matter how hungry I was, I had to have patience and not touch the food.

In Japan we did not show our emotions to people. No matter how hungry we were, we pretended we had had a big meal and we were full all the time. This we say *Bushi war kuwanedo takayougin. (*some samurai families were poor and did not have enough food to eat how hungry you were, you have to pretend you were not hungry). this was Japanese manners

I felt like my hands would come out from my mouth and try to grab the food, but I had to pretended and show her that I was not hungry, even though I had not had real good food for so long, also I was malnutrition with pregnancy.

She told me, "Please eat."

I said, "Thank you." Then I waited until she tried to offer me the food.

She said again “Please eat.” She repeated this a few times then finally she said, “Please eat before the food gets cold.” Then I allowed myself to eat.

Once I started to eat I forgot my manners. I opened my mouth as wide as I could and shoveled in as much food as I could. I tried to grab all the food without sharing with anybody. It seemed like somebody would try to take my food away. I tried not to let anybody take my food away. I was able to finish whatever food she put on the table. I was busy eating.

Then I realized she was watching me. I was embarrassing myself.

It was very delicious and I was so stuffed, that I couldn’t move at all. Then she tried to bring more food to me. I was in the heaven.

The first time I felt I was stuffed. I had been too long without food it took a lot of food to fill me up. I was emerging how much food I could put in my stomach looked like I had a hole in my stomach.

It was getting late in the afternoon. It was time to go home. I hated to leave her house. When I was in the door way, she told me, “I will cook nice Japanese food for you tomorrow. You come.”

I was so excited. I felt I had finally found my sister. I felt extremely happy. It gave me something to look forward to. I thought I would like to visit her regularly if I could. I didn’t want to end this little secret of mine and wonderful time I had.

On the way home I realized what kind of excuse I was going to tell Linda. While I was thinking on the way home I saw many lights from many houses. When I saw lights in these houses I remember my mother’s house. She had the same lights as Keiko’s neighbors that made me remember and made me more homesick. I knew that this time of the day, my mother’s house would have nice warm light and she would cook

Some wonderful food for me to eat.
How nice and how happy I was then. How deeply I missed her. I missed Japan! It made me crying.

I had enjoyed keiko's house as much as I could. I never occurred to me to come home on time for Linda and Betty's lunch.

When I arrived to Linda's house Linda and Betty were very upset. They spoke to me in loud voice and scolded me. They said I shouldn't go out of the house. They complained that they had to make their own lunches and had to take care of her baby. They chewed me up on and on. I felt that they were not going to stop!

I spent more time with Keiko. I got up in the morning and finished my chores then I tried to leave the house, but many times I did not succeeded.

When I was at Keiko's house, at least I could have some food to eat and speak Japanese.

She took me to the grocery store on the military base. We watched Japanese movies and she treat me special food to eat Japanese candy or pastry and drank miso soup. It was marvelous! I talked to Keiko about everything, especially my problems, but she did not give any advices. She was the only person who was someone I could trust and I could talk to besides my doctor.

Now Keiko knew my situation, and she really worried about my future baby and me.

She told me, "You should come to my house and eat as much as you need for your baby. I do not want to see you or your baby die. I can share my food with you and at least you enjoy it while you are here."

I swallow my tear. I must not cry. I am a strong Japanese woman.

One day when I was at Keiko's house my husband came to picked me up. He brought a bag of tomatoes with him and he try to give to Keiko. He was drunk. He tried to sit on the couch but he couldn't sit straight, and he smelled disgusting. He stayed at Keiko's house a little while than we left. (Around this time already Bob quit his job). this was the beginning of our problems and they get deeper and deeper as the day go by.

One evening Keiko and her husband took me to the officer's bar on the military base near our house. As soon as we sat down, before we enjoy a drink or relax. I noticed a drunken man with an angry face came toward our table. It was my husband Bob.

He was very nasty and he demanded I must go home with him. He was furious because I went to the officer's bar with my friend. I could see smoke come out from his head. Bob looked like ready to fight with Keiko's husband and he spoke very loud and rude.

I did not want embarrass Keiko and myself. I did not want to show his ugly behave to my friend.

When we got home, he showed me he was very angry and then his brother Sunny and sisters Betty, Nancy and Bob went out and left me home with Betty's baby, and Bob's three children.

I did not know where they went or how long they would be gone.

I couldn't understand why he was upset? I never believed I did something wrong. I thought I was stay home and taking care of children and clean house all time. Keiko took me to the officer's bar was fun experience. He did not had any problem his sister Betty took me to the bar. that the place was nasty, dark and dirty place, but officer bar was much clean and much better place to me. and I did not understand why he upset.

I love to go unknown place and see people have fun that make me enjoy and make me alive. I thought just sit down and talk to somebody or watch people have wonderful time I watch enjoying their life. I thought that was the wonderful time I would have. Why did you gave me hell and leave all the children with me and disappear? But I must try to be patience and obeyed like a good Japanese wife.

That was the only way I knew and I tried hard to understand his situation, but I did not like to see him drinking this heavily. I hated to see him become wasted and drunk person. It was painful to see him torn apart.

After this incident happened at the officer's bar Keiko never took me to the base anymore.

Few days after Bob stopped coming home regularly.

I remember, while we were having a lunch, Keiko told me "I teach you how to drive." I thank you for her kindness. I should appreciate, but I felt this is too much for her to teach me to drive. It was nightmare for me to study driving. I did study a book of driving before. Maybe driving was not my cup of tea.

One afternoon, I was tried to study drive exam, my husband and his sibling were at dining table in the Linda's house.

My husband's younger brother Kenney told me. "Kazuko, I teach you driving. "I felt, he really care about me and made me very happy.

I say "thank you," and I waited for him to speak. He asked, "What is a blinking light?" I was puzzled I hesitated to answer, but I said. "I don't know," with very seriously face.

He said, "It's a loose bulb" his sibling and Bob were laugh.

I was sad and felt dumb. Why you guys not take seriously about teach me or help me.

Keiko took me 7 times to the place to take the writing test for driving. I failed every test. Because the test was in English it was hard for me to understand the questions.

At the motor vehicle place everybody knew I had failed seven times. I felt they feel sorry for me. The eighth times I handed in my test. A lady from motor vehicle asked me to come to her desk.

I was scared my heart was beating very fast and my feet were trembling. My sweat run from my forehead and my body was shaking. I brought my answer paper to her and she went through it.

She asked me the question one at a time. If I gave her wrong answer she shook her head to let me know my answer was wrong. She asked me questions again. I correct my answer one by one.

I believed she wanted to help me to pass my test. It took us a long time to finish. After my interview with this lady finally I passed my test.

This time everybody from the motor vehicle congratulated me, and I was happy and proud.

I showed my passing exam to Keiko she told me, "Now you need to practice how to

Drive, and I will teach you. Don't you worry?"

She had a brand new car her husband had just purchased for her few days ago.

She took me to a location where nobody was there and she told me, "you come here from other side's door."

So I got out of the passenger door and got in the driver's side door.

She told me, "You start the car."

I knew I was a horrible driver and I knew I was going to bump and dent all over her new car. I was terrify. I positively knew this. I had no confidence about my driving. I hesitated to start her car.

She scolded me loudly, "you start the car" her voice startle me, I started the car.

I was so scared to give a gas. I tried touching gas pedal a little bit, the car was not move.

Keiko said, "Push gas pedal harder,"

I tried little bit harder, but the car wasn't move. Then she said, "Harder."

I tried but nothing happened.

Then she yelled at me, "Give more gas."

I step the gas to the floor then suddenly the car rush out very fast. I was panic. Sweat started running from my forehead. Oh my, I was terrified I thought my heart was going to stop. My blood was racing through my body. My hand was stuck like a chunk of wood to the steering wheel. My feet couldn't move left or right. I was stiff like a big tree was inside of me.

She said, "You are doing great, just keep go on"

"Really? Thank you for saying that, but I can't move at all." I say inside of my head. I tried whatever she told me to do.

Now she brought two garbage barrels. She puts one barren one side on the street and the other barrel same side street, but a distance apart from each other.

She shows me how to parallel park the car between the barrels.

I tried."Ops" I hit the front barrel, I tried to back. "Ops" I hit the back barrel. The car was stop and went. Then again and again bump and stop. Way I drive the car like a blind person walk on the street, never smooth. I did not know how many times I practiced back and forth. Finally I could park between the barrels. "Yapp."

Keiko was so happy she screamed and she jumped up and down clapped her hands.

I joined her and I found myself jumped up and down. We hug each other, jumped up and down. We laughed. We screamed. We looked at each other and we laughed so hard. Today was a good and wonderful day. (Middle of learning the driving, we were move to new place trailer park).

Finally it was time to take driving test.

I got into Motor Vehicle examiner's car. He wore uniform and spoke loud and short, when he looked at me made me panic. I tried to drive. But my feet did not move and my

Hands were stuck on the steering wheel like glue. My body was very stiff like a big tree grows from the floor. How I was frightened. I tried to listening what he said, but his pronunciation I couldn't understand and that made me more panic.

But somehow I started the car, When I finished drive, he looked at me and seem like he was disappointed my drive. I felt sad. Keiko taught me that I wasted her effort and time. And I was looking for some excuse to tell Keiko why I flunked the exam.

Then officer said." You pass the test. You will get a license."

I couldn't believe what examiner said to me just now. "Am I actually passed exam?"I pointed at myself with my finger and look at officer with wondering face. Still I couldn't believe what he just had said to me.

I showed Keiko with my new license. As soon as she saw, she held my hand and we jumped up and down and screamed again of happiness. I felt like I killed an enemy and I rewarded by the king. I was so proud. I wanted to show my license to my husband.

I thought that he would be proud of me and he thought what a smart wife he had. My thought was wrong. As soon as Bob saw my license he gave me a big black eye.

What a nice present? I did not want a black eye. I wanted him to be happy and proud of me. My dream was broken I was sad and angry. Why couldn't he be happy for me? I worked so hard to get this license. I was so disappointed and I didn't know how to explain to him. He did not want my explanation ether.

He smelled like alcohol and even he couldn't walk strait. Finally he went sleep mid afternoon.

Some little voice told me to take his truck's key and go for a ride. I obeyed this little voice.

It was dead sound. I tip toe walk very

careful make sure I did not wake him up. I was sweating. I hope he would sleep deeper and deeper. I felt adventure. I prayed he goes to sleep deeper and he won't to get up until I was able to sneak out the house.

My heart was racing. My hands were shaking.

Somehow I successful took a truck key from his pants. I went out with his key and I tried to drive his truck in the trailer park.

I knew I could drive Keiko's car, but I was afraid to drive his truck. This was new to me. I was scared, but I did drive the truck. I was so nervous my heart was pumping very fast.

I was driving around the park a little while. Here came to the end of the trailer park. All of saddened two poles show up.

One pole was electric wire and other was a water pipe. Was this truck too big? Was enough room to go through? Even me I could tell it was too narrow between poles. There was not enough space for the truck to go through. It was impossible.

What should I do? Should I leave his truck here and walk home or should I go through? I didn't know what to do, because I did not have enough knowledge about his truck how to back up, I was panic. Should I go through between the two poles?

Something told me go through between poles. Oh well let go through. My guess was right it was not enough for the truck.

I bent the poles and scraped the truck. I ripped poles and wires off and wires were all over lying on the ground. I made big damage.

I realized I could drive his truck maybe this would be the first and last time.

The little voice spoke to me again. "Go drive farther go." Oh well already I was in trouble why not. When I drive away something inside of me burst off.

I felt so good. Nice breeze chase me and the sun went home, and the moon came out to say hello to me.

It was a wonderful feeling I could drive far away. I forgot the time "Oops" it getting too dark now I should go home.

I did not know what was waiting at the house.

When I got home my husband was up. His hand was his hip and lean over in the door with angry face.

He seemed like a huge tree stand at the door no wind or nobody could move him away. I did not know trailer park manager complain to him about what I did. Well I have to deal with Bob.

Baby is born

Was I dreaming? I was in the hospital again with nervous breakdown. I was unconscious for three days that I was told.

This was my third time. My mental condition right now, is an angry, nasty storm that came and swept away all my good memories.

I didn't know how long I will be able to take or how many times more I will have to come back to this hospital as nervous breakdown, before my baby will be born. I hoped my mind will survive until then.

My baby's doctor Edward C took care of me very good. The doctor was not surprised to see me as sick as I was. As matter of fact, he was very concerned about my health. He worried about my labor and my mental exhaustion. I thought he could sense about my atmosphere in my home.

My emotional state was not good to having a baby, I believed. He could read the story of my life.

I was suffering my labor pains, but my baby was taking her time (I wanted a baby girl, so I decided I would have a girl). She had decided to give me more time made me anxious.

While I was in the hospital Bob took time off from his work to stay at hospital with me. It was nice. What a wonderful surprise! We had been married over one year.

I thought Bob wanted to meet our new family member. He acted so nice and sweet to me. I saw he was nervous about becoming a new father again.
Once again my baby was not ready to join her new family. Therefore, I went home for a few days after. I spend in the hospital a few days that helped me recovered a little bit from nervous breakdown. This happened around Christmas time. I felt home sick very badly especially around holiday time. It made me desperate to go home to Japan.

I remembered the times my family and we were together prepare for holiday event at my mother's house around this time of the year. My mother, my sister and her husband sat in the kotatu (a table with an electric heater built in and we put a blanket over the table). If I was home I would eat Japanese special holiday food and Japanese pastry. We drank a few cups of tea or even drink sake, or a coke. We would talk and laugh, and we would have super wonderful time.

Japanese pastry were resembled a flower or a bird. It is beautiful, it is a shame to eat, but we ate it anyway. the pastry is very sweet and delicious. We eat and drank tea and we talked until midnight. How deeply I missed this holiday.

When I think about this holiday time I can't stand to staying here in America. I wanted to go home right now.

Japan's (Osaka) winter is cold. Sometimes we have a snow. But everybody seemed happy, I imagine.

What I remember most about Japan was that all the family had together had an extraordinary time and we were happy. I wanted to go home. I wanted to go home right now. I wanted go home right at this moment. I thought I couldn't wait any longer to be backing home in Japan. I should go back to Japan long time ago. I should have my baby in Japan not here in America. I thought we would go back to Japan to have our baby. Now I realize we won't go back.

"Oh well" I said to myself, "I can't go home. I have to have my baby in this country. Whether I like or not, if I have my baby now, I want her to be a number one baby." It would be wonderful to have my baby at the first of the year. I 'm determined to have my baby on New Year's Day and make a new start to my American family I want her now. I have to have my baby on New Year day.

Conveniently my labor pain started again. Today is New Year's Eve and I have to go to hospital again. I think this is good. I will have a New Year's baby like I wanted. Will I have my baby tonight? How wonderful to have a first day of the year baby Maybe, it will happen I hope. My baby should be born on New Year's Day. May be it was too much to expected, but how wonderful if my baby is born on New Year's Day!

"Hey my future New Year's baby, Happy New Year to you, and you'd better been born this time. Don't be so lazy and stay in my stomach. I know you must be very nice and Conformable but you should be born tonight!" I talked to my baby, and I let my baby to know my intention.

Bob chartered a private air plane and he came to the hospital to visit me. What a nice husband! I felt, he really cared about me and our baby. He stayed with me in the hospital for a little bit and he left.

My baby decided not to be born this time again. I told the baby, "What a stubborn baby you are."

I told my husband about our baby, but he just smiles. He said, "The baby knows when it is time to be born. The time will come the baby will be born be patient."

Bob was very nervous but looked happy about our baby. His face just melted away like sweet candy.

I went home on New Year's Day with a big disappointment. This labor pain was a false alarm again. When I got home, I talked to my baby. "So you do not want to be born as I wish? Ok then. Be that way. I will be very stubborn like you." I talk to my baby.

I decided to take my time, as long as I needed, to make sure my baby won't trick ma again. January passes by, then comes Valentine's Day.

Now I wanted to have my baby on Valentine's Day. I felt pain again, or maybe I just thought because it was before Valentine's Day. Would I have my baby on Valentine's Day?

Somehow I start believe I will have my baby on Valentine's Day. I was so happy. I thought it will be a nice present for my husband, and I try very hard to have our baby on the Valentine's Day.

I am so happy to be having Valentine's baby. Maybe my dream will come true. Will this really the time my baby wants to be born or will she fool me again?

I went to the hospital. This was my third time. I was determined. I would have a baby this time definitely.

If I was in Japan, I would worship and walked outside of very narrow and hidden street (It was very secret place and from main Street couldn't see. This narrow street has a deep well on the end of one side of the street) from morning to midnight.

They dress in a thin kimono and walk about 20 feet. At the end of 20 feet had a deep well and inside of well had ice cold water and a bucket. They dump a bucket of ice cold water from head to toes then pray.

Whole body soaked. And then walk back to original start point. Back and forth dump cold water and walk again keep repeats this to the morning. They do this even cold winter snowing day.

Another way people go into ice cold very

strong waterfall and stood under waterfall and pray. Many people do this when they wanted something very much.

I did walk but without ice cold water.

I told my baby in my stomach. "Hey my baby girl, I really, really hope you are going to born this time. Do you hear me?"

When I arrive at the hospital that morning I am determined. I am going to have a baby this time definitely, but my baby seemed to settle in my stomach and made her comfortable again.

Next day when I saw my doctor I told him, "I won't go home until my baby born." The doctor winks at me. Then he tried to induce the baby that night. He told me, "You have to walk in the hospital as much as you can."

As soon as I heard this, I started to walk from the first floor to the second floor and then the third floor. Upstairs and downstairs I walked all night. It was uncomfortable and painful. It was so hard to walk through the hospital all day and all night. Then I noticed there was the water I did not remember how much water was, but I felt it was all over the Floor, and I saw some water dripping down the stair.

I notice a maintenance man had a mop and he followed after me to wipe my water.

My doctor had broken my water to help my baby to be born quickly. I did try all the hard work to help my baby to be born. Did this hard work help my baby to be born? It was a painful experience. I noticed that my pains became deeper and deeper. It was pains, terrible pain. I couldn't stand anymore. Also I couldn't walk anymore. I was scream in the hallway and I tried to grab anybody came near me. I screamed and screamed. I felt my screams would take my pain away. I screamed and screamed and screamed. all I could do was scream! I screamed at my doctor. "Do something to make my pain go away." I kept screaming until my voice wouldn't come out anymore.

Finally I was on the bed and waiting for my baby to come.

I swear to whoever entered my room, "go away" I was a terror. I was miserable. I was misbehaver. I was in excruciating pain and embarrassed myself by scream and shout.

Finally my baby was born. The baby was born two days after Valentine's Day. February 16. "Oh shucks!"

This time, unfortunately, Bob couldn't take a day off. That was why I had to have a baby alone. I felt something was missing. I felt a lot of disappointment and was very sad. It was miserable to be by myself. I wish my husband was here.

I saw another new mother getting many flowers and many visitors. Her husband held his new baby. He was smiling and happy. The whole family surrounded the new mother and baby with big smiles. They were looking at the baby and this new mother has warmly a lot of supportive from their families and happy.

When I saw her and her family it made me jealous. I wished my husband was here. He should be here to join his new family, not before my baby born.

I told myself, *"He came back here a few times before baby born, and he stay with me. I should know he cared about me and new baby so don't be jealous."* But I needed him right at this moment. I needed his support and I wanted to hear him say that we had a beautiful baby.

I was so disappointed. I felt very isolated. I felt scared and sad. I wanted him to hold our new family member.

After baby was born my doctor came to my room.

I asked him, "Is my baby a boy or a girl?"

He said "A beautiful boy."

I told the doctor with disappointed voice, "You told me I would have a girl. You should take this baby back and switch for a girl."

He smiled and he said "All right." Then he walked away and disappeared.

"*You shouldn't walk away you should take seriously what I say*." I wanted to call after him. That was what I thought. I was little angry and not happy when that Dr walked away from me "Who do you think I am talking to you? Don't you walk away in the middle of the conversation?" I talk only to myself, but after I saw my baby, I understood why he laughed and he disappeared.

When I saw my baby he was a beautiful baby boy to me. I was not disappointed one bit. However Edward had a lot of winkles and a lot of black hair all over him like a monkey.

I named my baby Edward because it was my doctor's first name as well as my husband's middle name. He was so tiny I am afraid to hold him. I was no education how to raise a baby, and I never thought I would be a mother. I did not have mother nourishment in me.

Linda came to the hospital. She told me, “The baby is a boy and he is very beautiful.”

She said, “He has five fingers and five toes. He looks a very health boy.”

I listened to her but I did not understood what she really means. When she told me my baby was beautiful? *Did her really thinking my baby was beautiful. I thought my baby was just another baby to her, like many other strangers’ babies. When she told me that my baby was beautiful,* It was big surprise to me.

I was in my hospital bed. Each time door was open I was so excited maybe this time was my husband. I thought, he finally able to take day off and came home to see me. I dreamed my husband was home. My expectation was so high and I got disappointed very deeply.

Another night Betty came to my room in the hospital. She brought me a dark red color close to black color a rose. I thought that was a nice present that cheered me up a little bit, and I wanted to believe she cared about me and my baby. She stayed only a few minute to keep me company but while she was in my room she never mention about my baby not even once. Did she wonder my baby was a boy or a girl? I didn't know if she saw my baby or not.

She told me, "I have to go, I am still working." She yawned and shouted. She left my room very quickly.

Her action made me thought about whether she was not cared about my son that made me disappoint.

At feeding time a nurse brought my son to my bed. He was so tinny, and he trusted me to hold him. What a cute baby.

I looked at him with joy and happiness and tried to make him comfortable and I Let him know I was his new mother I will do anything to make you happy, I thought. What a treasure.

When I was eager to breast feed my baby the first time, I found out I Couldn't feed my son. My milk dried out, surprise! I was in panic and I didn't know what happened to me. "Am I crippled? Why couldn't I feed him?" I was devastated, and I cry. I couldn't feed my baby? Why I couldn't feed him? My heart was torn. I found out later why my milk was dry out.

The next day when my doctor comes to my room, I tried do a handstand in the bed. I was doing excise.

He saw me and he said, "It is too soon to be doing exercises. Wait a couple more days." Then he asked me "Is everything all right?"

I say "I think so

He says, "The baby is healthy. I think he won't have any problems. Do you want to go home?"

All of a sudden it hit me, do I have to go home? His word brought me back to reality.

Why couldn't I stay away Linda's home forever? I didn't want to go home to Linda's house. Why couldn't I return to my home in Japan? But I said "I guess so" with shadowed voice.

He told me, "If any problems happen to you or your baby call me. I will give you my private number." When he walked away I could sense his concern for me. I wondered if he guessed what my life was like.

I realized that he was the only person I trusted since coming to America.

When I think about going back to Linda's house my stomach started pain and throw up. My feet felt heavy like a chain attached to big solid metal ball that's wrapped around my leg. I got goose pimples all over and started shaking. My tears rushed out from my eyes and dripping on the hospital gown, my gown was soaked.

Time passed by so quickly when I was in the hospital. Then I realize time to go home, but I did not want.

My sister-in-law Betty was so eager to get me home.

She told the Doctor, “kazuko had to go home immediately.”

However, my doctor winked at me and he told Betty, “She is not yet strong enough to go home.”

The doctor made sure I could stay a few more days. He saved me. What a relief! While I was in the hospital, my doctor tried to getting touch with the welfare people. After he did everything he could think of to help me, then he released me to go home. I think my doctor thought I would be all right when welfare people come to my house. He thought they would help me.

I went back home and a few weeks passed. A middle aged fat man with square face who worked for social services, came to my house.

I remember what he said to me, "You should go back to Japan. We will take care of your baby for you."

I asked him to repeat this to me again. I wanted to make sure I was not misunderstanding what he said.

I repeated his words to myself very slowly to make sure I understood him. "I go Japan. You take my baby?"

He agreed with big smile.

Rage fills me. My face was red as fire, my body shakes my tears run down. I scream at him. "Go!" I pointed him to the door, and I said, "Go! Leave my house right now! You never come here again!" Before I finished my words shouting out, he run out my house and he drove away as quick as he can. I still shake. My mind was so confused and upset. I couldn't find any other words to say. I mumble to myself as I walked back and forth in my room to calm down. It took a very long time for me to calm down.

I did not understand why government would take a baby away from mother? In our country never happens.

Few weeks after, Bob's grandmother was visiting Linda from Massachusetts for few weeks. She came to my room while I change the baby's diaper.

She insisted on teaching me how to change a diaper. When she took off Edward's dirty diaper, she smiled at him. She opens her mouth big as she can, here comes baby's number one going to her mouth perfectly, it's a home run. She ran to the bathroom.

I laughed. I laugh as hard and loud as I could. I thought that my voice ran through the house to my neighbors. They could hear my laughing voice.

It was so funny to me the way she made a face and then run into the bathroom.

I thought "you do not need to show me

how to change a diaper." But I dare not tell her.

When Bob comes home, Linda told him what Edward did to Bob's grandmother. He just laughed.

He had a very contend and happy face. We were still having wonderful times and he was still good, kind and nice man to me.

Linda came up with an idea as usually. "You put baby's crib into your bedroom." Her explanation was, "You can keep an eye on the baby better." Her sound seemed like very sweet and care, but our bedroom was very small. There was no room to walk between our bed and the crib. I had to walk on the bed to reach the crib.

In middle of night I got up and went to the kitchen to get baby formula. Each time I saw the baby's bottle, my heart tears apart. We Japanese women breast feed their babies that is very important. If woman couldn't breast feed the babies, people felt she was not a good mother and not respectable. That she was incapacitated and she was a big failure. We believed these women who couldn't breast feed, she was a cripple. She must have done something very bad her life or before her life. For example, she treated people very bad, lie, steal or made people suffer, so now her turn to payback what she did. God punishes her.

Long after I came back home from the hospital I found out that while I was in the hospital, Linda had told a nurse, "Kazuko is going to use formula for her baby." Therefore, the nurse gave me a shot so my milk would not develop while I was pregnant.

She never told me what she done to me I had no idea such a thing existed. I was very upset and sad. Why did she decide a very important thing like breast feeding without asked me? Did I have any choice about how to raise my son? Breast feeding was very important to me.

I keep asking myself "why didn't she ask me? This is entirely opposite of what I believe to raise my baby. Either Bob or Linda ever ask me about how I want to raise my son or how I feed my baby. How I rise my baby was my concern. Why did Linda interfere?

Many horrible things would happen if I listened to Linda. What I thought was I did not want her to make any decisions about my son. I wanted to take care of Edward good as I could. I hope to have nothing to do with Linda. She could see Edward, when I was with him if she wanted. I hope I won't be forced to let her tell me how to raise my son. To me my son is my life. I care the best for him. I will live my life for my son and his future. I won't let anybody to hurt my son. He will be safe and happy with me. I will decide what the best for Edward.

Quite while after baby born, Bob did not talk to me much anymore. When he sat at dinner table, he was depressing. He had quite few times showed me he was saddened. Dumb of me I couldn't realize what happened to him. After dinner Bob told me, "I am going to quit my job."

His announcement was surprises me! I asked, "Why? I thought you enjoyed your job very much also we were looking forward to go back to Japanese company to work.

I do not understand why?" I was hoping this was not true. I hope he was just saying that. He said to me "my mother told me I should change my job, because I marry to you, and we have new one in our family. I coming home every other weekend am not fair for you. I should find a new job where near our home so I can coming home every day. I should stay home with you."

I was surprised! I told him, "Please do not quit your job because of me? I can handle situation and I can take care of three children good. Now many Cuban are move into

Florida and it is hard to get any job even how talented you are." But my wish was defeated by his mother's demand. Bob made me realized how strong Linda's influence was. He already had quit his job. What a pitfall.

After he quit his job our life were roll down to the downhill very fast and very bad.

I was amazed about Linda, how manipulated and control woman. Why she had to use me as good excuse about change his job? Why? Why had he obeyed her and quit his wonderful job? I did not understand at all. Would she try to make his life to hell? Did she care about him and his future? It was too much puzzle to me.

Maybe did she know we were talking about going back to Japan? If he stay same job we would back to Japan soon.

His company wanted him. Especially Japanese company, they would situated him good housing. And they would paid does not matter how much cost them. Bob was a very valuable person to Japanese company.

I know, Linda knew how intelligent her son and how valuable person he was. I did not understand why? Why did she try to control him? I hope she care about her son's future. Seem liked she tried tie his neck with a lope and hold on it. Why did she convince my husband to change his excellent jog?

When he tried to change his job, obviously he lost job. Then he became drunk very heavy than before, but I saw, he was trying very hard to find any job. He tried to be a good provider to his children and his mother as he used to be. But many jobs were taken by Cuban. He was depressing every day.

I just watch him was so painful and so sad. I was not able to help him. I wish I could, but I couldn't I hated feel that I was in despaired. I saw my husband changing, and he became total wasted drunker. I hated to see him like this, but what can I do? Our life was gone to hell? I thought maybe I didn't speak English well. I felt that why I couldn't help Bob and I couldn't communicate with Linda.

I discuss with Keiko before. "I wanted to learn English and speak better."

She said, "I will show you where the school and you could register to take English classes." I remembered that she said to me.

I remembered I was excited and very happy. I thought, "I need that. That was my whole problem. If I could speak English well maybe his family treat me better and I could understand American way." Finally I got my answer what to do."

Keiko's information gave me hope. Hooray! My problem was over. I felt like jumped around, and I would like to fly. When Linda saw I was smiling, that made her mad again.

I asked my husband when he was home at Linda's house. At that time we were still lived with Linda. I was with full prided and I asked to Bob, "Is all right to go to school? Would you watch Edward while I go to school?"

Linda said "Why do you think you need to learn English?" Then she said to me, "He can speak to you in Japanese and we do not have any problem. You keep speaking Japanese. If you do not understand a chore Bettye and I will help you."

I was shock. I told myself. *"Don't you want me to speak English better?"* But I did not ask them why. I just shut my mouth and I question myself why they said that. Like a little girl, she lost her most precious toy or something very important, and she lost her dream. I looked down on the ground to make sure my husband did not see my face.

Then I realized, I felt, how much important to me to understand English especially if I was stay in the U.S.A. I persisted begging him until finally he say, "all right, and all right.

Stop saying you need English, go head go to school" with irritated voice.

Linda said, "I wonder how long you will last." Then she walked away from me.

Her action as if I give her some disease.

I didn't care what they say or how they felt.

When I heard his approval, all of sudden dark cloud lifted up and I saw tinny light peaked out from the cloud.

I was so happy! "Yes I can go to school." Oh how wonderful to be in the School, and I could speak English like other people and actually I would understand English. I knew, I will study hard and I will be a best student.

Words flow out from my mouth. Seem like I tried to convince him. From now on I will be smart and I will be able to learn American way? I was excited.

I ask him, "would you coming home my school day?"

He says, "I have to haven't I." His voice was very irritated.

I did not realize at that time how upset he was.

I prepared myself for first day of the school. I changed my clothe one to another and looked in mirror. I changed again. Was this clothing respectable for school or maybe another clothe better? How was my hair do Was my hair style good enough? Did I have everything need for school? The butterfly flew in my stomach jumped up and down. I was so nervous, but I was excited.

I was so busy myself I did not realize no one was the home to help me to go to school. I waited to Bob to coming home. I waited to 5:00 pm nothing happen. Then I waited to6:00 pm. I heard sound of car I rushed to the window to see who was. There was some stranger but not Bob. I waited a while no sound. I started to walk to school with my son. It took me more than two hours of walking. I did not have a baby carriage so I have to carry my baby with one hand and the baby diaper bag with other hand. I was so anxious to learn English.

When I got the school people were left and school was closes. I was disappointed. I cried and I cried. I got discourage very deeply. I knew I needed to learn English. Anything I wanted to do in this country or to better understand America I must learned English. On the other hand Linda and Betty work so hard to make sure I couldn't go to school. I couldn't understand why did they keep me dumb? Didn't they want to be proud of me when I become smart?

Betty left her baby with me and never come back until after my school was over. I had to clean the house. Linda would leave me some work to do, and watched Bob's children. His family made sure I could not continued school. I hated to give up school. Give up was not me. I did not want to quite. But thing were not as they promised at all.
I really wanted to become a better person.

I would do how hard or how long would take me I was ready to learn. I was sad and disappointed about Bob's family treated me. All of sudden my entire dream which I buildup was tore down to small pieces. I was so desperate.

I should know I won't get help, but I asked Linda anyway. "Would your watch my son and take me to the school?"

She said to me, "That is your husband's business. If he did not come home than you should stay home and not bother to learn English. Anyway, you won't able to lean with your brain."

Now I knew they did not want me to go to school. I felt they were value me as stay home and taking care of his sister's baby and Bob's kids. Do clean the house and cook that all I was good for and also they didn't speak proper English to me they said like "go" or "eat" speak just verb not collect sentence that did not help my English grow. I felt I was so useless and sad. I did not understand why people tried to keep me dumb? So much different people were here America then Japan?

One day we were at kitchen table, he told me he had sole his house. Few weeks after I found out he bought brand new two bedroom double size trailer for his mother and brand new three bed room trailer for his sister and used three bedrooms trailer for us, and we stayed in the same trailer park. (How convenient for them! also Linda's explanation was because of us made them to move)

While I was listening his information, I felt like I was listening somebody's conversation, and I never felt this was us. I just did not understand this situation at all.

We were moved to our trailer in the trailer park. I thought I could live different place and separate from his mother I would have some freedom.

Even used trailer to me this is my home and this is my castle. I would like to take this used trailer. I couldn't ask more than happy. I did not realize Linda's determination.

I thought we had a happy married, but time passed by we got very depress and had change Bob's personality a lot.
I did not know my husband was paying all trailer park fees too.

Only worry me how could I go to Keiko's house and I wanted to keep our friend ship, if I was moved to new place it was much farther for me to walk with baby. I did not see her after eddy was born.

After we moved to trailer park, Linda came to my trailer without calling me. She said, "I saw your husband with some other lady and looks very happy. Why was he not happy with you?"

I did not like to hear or did not want any information about my husband.

I thought back now she used her information to make me like a dog lost the war and put the tail between the legs and covered my face running back to Japan. Where I would no longer to be a threaten to her that I thought, but she did not want to care for his children so I was necessary for her. There for She enjoying putting me down.

I was so beaten down by her words. Please do not make less of me.

Bob knew I was hurting. Even thought Bob joined a motorcycle group. He bought a new jean jacket, he stepped it and spill beer on that jacket. He made new jacket into a dirty disgusting jacket. He ride motorcycle and drink all day and he disappeared few days with many different girls. When he came home he was drunk and he tried pick on me for so little thing.

After Edward was born I had nervous breakdown again. When I woke up in the hospital I was so sick. I did not know what happened.

I believed the incident that was after I feed Edward I gave a bath I changed his diaper I put clean clothes on him and I put him on the couch I fell down on the floor. I didn't know how long I was unconscious. The next door neighbor found the smoke started form our house made her suspicious. When she found me on the floor she called the ambulance then ambulance took me to the hospital. When I woke up I was in the hospital bed. I had unconscious three days that I was told.

Betty came to the hospital she said, "A fire started your trailer in the kitchen this fire almost burn down the kitchen. The next door lady called the fire department. Eddy was on the couch"

I did not remember that I washed Eddy or changed diaper but I made sure my son was all right. I wanted to keep him in a safe place and then I fell down? I put him in clean clothe no matter how sick I was I always think of my son's safety. The mother's love is so strong. I realized.

This happen was after my doctors released me and send me home.

Now I really didn't know what to do. I knew I couldn't and I won't to stay home here if I do stay here I will get sick again. The mental and emotional pressures also the way they treated me make me suicidal.

Only my love for eddy kept me strong and gave me courage. I had to get out of this house away from these people who were doing dangerous to my health and my well being. That why I did run away from the house but that was fail and I came back to our trailer.

In Japan when woman married. The wife's job was to carry his family's name well and proud to be a husband's wife. His children would have his name.

In some part of Japan, a long, long time ago in the country side of Japan. Husband's quest visited him husband would offer his wife to his quest without asking the wife. In Japan was man's world and woman were servants of him and his family. In Japan society is contradiction.

I was born to a Samurai family and rise in the old fashioned strict Japanese system. Ancient Japanese blood was running through my body, but I tried to live the new wave of Japan. I was caught between two different cultures.

My husband's mother treated me terrible more than any Japanese mother in- law.

In Japan a good wife is, not seeing, not heard and not talked. Therefore, I took Linda's treatment very well, I didn't have any problem with the way she treated me.

Nevertheless, Linda was an extremely negative person. To me she was a devil from core. Her brain is mixed up. She showed me a terrifying person to me.

I realized she was a very talented person. Who can give misery to other people? Her action did not bother me bet and I have much patient.

I thought Linda hated to see me, when I laugh or I have a good time. When Linda come my house she never knocked our door. She just opened the door and storm in. As soon as she came in my house she started scold me down with fury voice with ghostly looked.

When I saw her goose pimples all over in my body, and I have to listen her nick picking,

she always looked something to complain. She was a very good for that. She was a chubby woman, but when she started pick on me, made her bigger than ever. Her stern voice that she won't give me any space to run and put me in a corner and made me stifles. She made my place become a dudgeon.

She asked me, “Why Bob’s children were misbehaved.”
Why. Why. Why? Every day she said to me.

Make sure she let me know how much she detested me. That made me sad.

Each time she tells me I’m wrong for. I always said to her, “I am so sorry I will try harder. I hated myself how I became useless and powerless.

Move to Massachusetts

September in the Florida was still humid and hot. It was 5:00 am outside our trailer park was still dark and quiet, and it was a little cool. People were not up yet. I could hear wind whistling. Seem like very quiet like before tornado start. It was a very silent morning.

I sat at the kitchen table. I put my coffee cup down on the table. I just had made wonderful warm coffee. It smelled marvelous and refreshing. To surprise, my husband was sitting across from me and having a cup of coffee with me. It was an extraordinary surprise.

We hadn't had a cup of coffee, nor had a dinner together, for so long. This was so awesome and nice treats for me. It was good to have someone to share the good taste of fresh, wonderful coffee and it made my coffee taste much better.

My husband told me "I sold our trailer. We have to pack up as much we can. We are going to move out of here and away from Florida tomorrow."

He said this with a rusty voice and with no emotion. His face was like old flimsy paper, if touch ready to tear up into small pieces. He looked exhausted. He looked like a very, very, very, old man to me. He was no longer the same man I married. His face looked like a dead person. I saw him nothing left inside. His eyes looked at the air not focusing. I could tell, He was trying to avoid me. When I heard the sorrow in his voice, it was so painful, that I could not watch him.

He was torn too much, and he was very beaten down deeply. I could only watch my coffee cup. I watched the steam come out of my cup. My eyes followed the curls as it went up to the ceiling and disappeared like my dream. I hugged my cup so tight I broke the cup. I did not know how to talk to him or what to say to him anymore, I was lost.

I did not want to offend or damage him. I did not want him to think I was a fool. Did I remember what kind of conversation pleased him? I did not know the words anymore. I just couldn't think. I felt so isolated from everyone. I was alone in this very big and strange country.

I did not know when my husband sold our trailer and to whom. Was I allowed to say something about the sale of our trailer? Was I allowed to say my feelings about moving? Did I have a right to express my opinions? Would my opinion be important to him? There was no reason to arguing with him.

I hoped I could have more time. I needed more time to prepare for moving. I just couldn't do a good job with one day to do clean the house and pack all our stuff. I needed to sort the stuff to give away or bring with us. Also I had to say goodbye to my neighbor. Even with a small trailer it was too much to do all this works in a day.

He told me "I got $500." I did not understand if he had $500 for travel expenses or did he have any money left for after we arrive to destination? I knew $500 was not enough money to fine new place to live and for our trip.

He had never told me his financial situation before. I did not know why he had sold it for so little money. Why was he trying to give away our house? Was he running away from law? Was he running away from something or hiding from everybody? What was happed to him? What was he thinking? I wished I know what was his intention?

Maybe he heard my incident I had run away from our trailer? Maybe he realize about his mother and his sibling? Maybe he thought if we moved away from here we would have better our life? I wished he would talk to me. Made my mind was full wonder.

I stopped thinking and started to pack. I would make some food to take with us when we would leave here tomorrow.

While I was packing, he did not say a word to me. He just looked at me like I was a stranger to him. His face was blank and motionless like a brittle, old, dead tree knocked down by a soft wind. Maybe he had lost his words, just like I had lost the music in my heart.

He did not say if he would have a job or not. He did not tell me, if we would have a place to stay when we arrived in Massachusetts. I wish he would tell me.

I wanted believe we have a place to live

and we would have the wonderful life will wait for us. Everything would be awesome, “but realty” I was confused and scared. What next? When would it be over, my entire pointless life? I was exhausted and disappointed.

When we finished this move, I hope I would not have to pack and unpack my few items anymore. I hope.

It took me very little time to pack our items especially mine. I owned one sundress. I had made this dress when I was in Florida. My personal items filled less than one small paper bag. I was amaze. When I came to the United States, I brought a lot of my personal things from Japan. But now I realized there was very little left. All my clothes, handbags, jewelry, our wedding picture, and many other items were gone. How could I live with so few things? I thought homeless people had more clothes than I had. Even my shoes were gone. There was only one pair of sandals left, the one I was wearing.

When I was a young girl, I used to own many designer shoes, designer clothes and designer handbags. I grew up with nice, rich and tasteful of things surrounding me, and I loved it. I had enjoyed my life extremely well, but now I had only one bag and pair of shoes and sundress left.

I packed everything except a few dishes and few things. I took just what I would need for that night a few blankets, pillows and towels, some soap, a few cooking pans and dishes and some changes of clothes for my son.

I knew we had to leave the next morning. There was no time for me to complain.

I did not know if Bob's children were to stay in Florida or not. I did not ask questions any more. I knew by now that I wouldn't get any answers from them. I felt like no longer existed. I felt useless. Had I forgotten who I was? Wasn't I allowed to express my feeling? Was I afraid to articulate my feeling?

I had put my feelings in a little box and tied it around with a rainbow ribbon and put away in a corner of my heart. I hoped someday I could open it. I hoped that day will come. I started to learn how to behave myself around them. Did I have the right to ask questions? Did I have any choices? I just did whatever they wished. I was numb.

I started packing my husband's clothes. I Was amazed how many clothes he had compared to my son and me. It took me a whole day to pack his clothes. He had beautiful suits, jeans, T-shirts and many shoes. I wish my husband would help me with this packing to tell me which one he would bring with him and which one he would leave here. I wished his children would help me too.

"*What a dreamer I was*!" I knew, I could not get help from them. I knew that it wouldn't happen. "*Give up thinking, they* *won't help me."*I thought but deep inside me I had hope that someday they would help me. I still wanted to have hope: I still wanted to believe in them. I was such a fool!

After I finished packing, I started cleaning the inside of our trailer corner-to-corner. I made sure everything was clean. I did not want to leave a dirty place. I worked extra hard for new dweller. We (Japanese) keep place absolutely clean for new people that were our custom.

I started to scrub the floor on my hands and knees. I did not own any cleaning solution. This was how I did it. I put water in a little plastic bowl with a little soap in it and I polished the floor. I put my knees on the floor and I scrubbed. It became shinning not like rust wore out junk yard metal when we moved in. When I washed the floor, I used an old rag. I had used it so many times it was worn out. Then I threw it out. As I scrubbed I looked at our shinning floor.

I used to think people never changed, but now how I had changed.

When I was In Japan, I acted like a clown and I had full energy and full life. I made many, many my friends laugh and made them happy, but I was a shy person until I get know people. When I open my mouth, usually I made my friends laugh tremendous because of laugh, I saw some people had tears in their eyes, and I was always acting like a comedian to them. When I started to speak to my friends, I did not know when or how to stop. My words came out of my mouth like I was started singing a song and, before I finished one song, I started singing another new song.

Also I was a very stubborn and self-confident person. I loved to talk. I loved to make people laugh. I loved to see other people laugh and happy.

I was a center in the group and I demanded to be everybody should be happy. I enjoyed seeing people having a good time and being happy. I was full live and I loved it. Now I had lost my wards. I had become a scared, dead person. I worked like a little ant and kept going until it was very dark outside.

I did not know about Massachusetts. What did it look like in Massachusetts? Was the weather cold or hot there? Did they have flat land like Florida or mountains? Were there many different kinds of people living there? Did they have four seasons? Did they have public transportation like Japan? Did many Japanese people live there? How for from here to Massachusetts?

Question came to my mind like water running from the kitchen faucet. The unknown made me scared of what would happen next. I had had a plenty of experience with misfortune in this country. I hoped my life wouldn't be too bad there in Massachusetts.

I kept telling myself I should not be scared anymore. "Scared" was not my style. I was a strong woman. I was Japanese. I was a stubbed. I had spirits and courage. It was just another strange place to live, with many new strange people. I shut up. Any hard jobs were not hard for me anymore, because I had built up toughness during lived with Linda.

Linda wanted me to work for their family and take care of Bob's three children without any communication. My word was not good for them. They did not want to talk to me. They commanded me to do thing for them, but they did not want to listen what I said to them. She always paid a lot of attention to looking for my mistakes. She always calls me "You are such a lazy woman, a lazy bum or here come a lazy bum." To front of everybody and they were laughing when they heard Linda call me lazy bum. I thought "lazy bum" was a friendly word and it was kind humored. Now I know I was ignorant.

Let me tell you how I grew up in Japan. My Japanese house was sparkling. Our wood hallways were always shining if you did not pay attention, when you walk on the wood floor you would slip and fall on your butt. And any tinny litter or trash was never found inside of the house. It was super clean. For example dogs were not allowed to stay inside of the house because dogs were went outside there for their feet were dirty.

When people came to the house they took their shoes off and washed their feet before going to hallway onto the main floor.

The entrance to Japanese house, there is a small hallway (usually cement or stone floor) where shoes are left before stepping up into the house. Between the floor and the main house have a big stone or a wood for step. You step up this stone or wooden step and sit on the main hallway.

There was a bowl of water and a new towel beside of the bowl.

People sit down wood floor and wash their feet before step up to the main house. Each time wash feet owner of the house make sure change to clean water and new towel left for new guest. This was my mother's house when I grow up.

I remember when my son was before two years old we visited my sister's house in Japan. My son came down stair with eating some cookie. My sister's helper was behind him hold vacuum cleaner to pick up any crumb he drops. She explain to me she wash the floor twice a day and clean the house every day.

I thought scrubbing a floor was not my style. I never thought of cleaning my house, and I refused to do such a dirty jog. Also I couldn't touch any dirty thing or go near any dirty place. When I saw or touched dirty stuff and dirty smell I threw up.

I always told my mother "When I grow up and I own a house, I will hire somebody to clean my house, just like you or my sister. You have someone to clean your house, cook and do all kinds of house work. So will I.

I was a typical young girl, smart mouth and obnoxious. I never thought of cleaning the house or doing chores. That was not my job. We always had someone to take care of our chores. Maybe sometimes I would tried to cook food for just fun.

I used to do some weekend, I drove to hot spring and bathe myself to bask. Maybe I would take a few days trip to see something new place or see some play and visiting museum to see wonderful art or go tea ceremony or go to see *kabuki*(Japanese play dress up very old fashion style just like opera in this country).

I always enjoy my life extremely good and happy, and I would have helper for my house to take care and cleaning and cooking for me. That I though what a dreamer I was!

Now I scrubbed the floor and cleaned our place. Especially I cleaned our trailer. While I cleaned I did not think of any problems. I did not think about what might happen or what would be tomorrow. My mind was at peace It took me awhile to finish cleaning. After I finished cleaning, I sat on the couch. I looked around at the inside of the trailer and I felt good.

I hoped whoever bought this trailer would enjoy it and take good care of it. I hoped whoever moved into this trailer would be happy and have a good life.

I sat on the couch and looked around the room. So many memories were here. It was like I was looking at many movies, one

Memory to after another rushed out of my head, but not one memory could be called a pleasant memory. I should leave all my memories in this trailer. I should not take these memories with me. All my memories were very bad and sad. Now thinking back, there were nothing good memories, but, the funniest thing was, even the bad memories now seemed to be not so bad.

As I thought, I did not know how my life had ended up like this. Did I take a wrong turn? Didn't I pay attention to what was going on? I wasn't sure.

I always wanted to have good times and be happy. I liked to eat and live well. Worry free! I all times wanted to have a great time. When or where I wanted to go I could go free like a bird. I thought my life will be always have good time and happy.

Many people called me "dream girl." I had so much hope and big dream when I was young. I had hard time and not happy life in America, even so I would not regret, what happened here. Maybe something was missing in my life? Maybe I must learn something. Was this a part of my lessons? I thought, I had not wasted any time here but I had almost forgotten what a normal life was like.

I was the first person to get up in the morning when the outside was still dark, and I was the last person to go to bed. I did not have a minute to sit down and relax. Was I allowed or was I deserved to be enjoy a moment of peace and quiet? I should leave my entire memoir here.

Bob and I and our son, we were going to have a new life. "A better life." I hope. We would make a new life together with my husband and us. I hoped maybe we could start all over and start to talks each other. I hoped we would have a better life there in Massachusetts. Hope... Hope... Hope.

When I realized it was already getting light outside. I have to go to bed still I had got a few hours of sleep. I got up and made a pot of coffee and a breakfast for Bob and his children. I put the breakfast on the table. I woke Bob and his children up. While they were eating, I fed my son. After breakfast, His children were disappeared. I thought they were just went out and play. I did not found out what happen to them or where did they go? I did not have time to look after them.

I washed and wiped the dishes and put them in the box. I brought the box out to the station wagon and gave it to Bob.

The old and rust station wagon, We were going to travel from here to Massachusetts, the future place, with this old, unreliable car?

I did not understand what had happen to my husband. Once he always had a new beautiful car.

I went back into the trailer while he put the box in the station wagon.

I stood inside the trailer and I looked around inside, and I spent a moment. This was my last chance to check and the last time to look at my miserable life. I hoped.

My new life would be much better. It had to be! A new life where we could laugh and we could talk to each other. I would cook, and we would sit down to have dinner together. Maybe we would sit down and watch television together. Maybe we could go for walks together.

We would make a wonderful, caring, cherishing and enchanting new life together. I hope. We would be all right. We would make a better life there and be happy like we used to be in Japan. Life couldn't be bad all time. Someday, the sun would come out from the dark stormy clouds and bring us bright sunshine. Hope, the bright sunshine, would be there to light up all over me, to greet me, and to hold me softly and bless me in our new life. I wanted to believe all the bad times were over. Good times would have to come. A Good life will be there and waiting us when we arrived in Massachusetts.

Was I dreaming? Who was I trying to kidding? Let hope let me think good things will be there. Hope this is the end of our miserable life I needed a wonderful dream, and I needed to believe we will be all right when we arrived in Massachusetts. I hoped we will start a wonderful new life there. I had to believe.

I walked through the kitchen to children's bed rooms, and went to our bed room to make sure I had not missed any dirty spot. I did not like to leave any dirty place for new owner, for their new life. I walked through the trailer with mixed feelings.

In this trailer I spent less than one year, but sure too many sad thing had happen. It is hard to believe. Well I hope the best. We will leave with the old rust unreliable station wagon this afternoon from Florida to Massachusetts. Good luck to me. We pack personal staff in the car also we had a so little money. Even though, my son had fever, he was so quite while we drive always to Massachusetts.

When we arrive in Worcester I found out Bob had rented one bedroom apartment with furniture. I was astonished when and how he could do while we were in Florida. This place will start our new life and good life. I hope........